MACMILLAN ACADEMIC SKILLS

Skillful

Reading & Writing

Teacher's Book

4

Authors: Stacey H. Hughes & Lara Storton
Series Consultant: Dorothy E. Zemach

Macmillan Education
4 Crinan Street
London N1 9XW
A division of Macmillan Publishers Limited
Companies and representatives throughout the world

ISBN 978-0-230-43012-9

Written by Stacey H. Hughes and Lara Storton

First published 2014

Designed by emc design limited

Cover design by emc design limited

Page make-up by MPS Limited

The Academic Keyword List (AKL) was designed by Magali Paquot at the Centre for English Corpus Linguistics, Université catholique de Louvain (Belgium) within the framework of a research project led by Professor Sylviane Granger.

http://www.uclouvain.be/en-372126.html

Authors' acknowledgements

Stacey Hughes

Many thanks to John, Juliet, and Sara for their support and encouragement.

Lara Storton

My appreciation and thanks go to my colleagues over the years at the UUNZ School of Business, Auckland, Australian School of English, Perth, and Hilderstone College, U.K., who have provided a wealth of invaluable teaching ideas and support; and to my fantastic students who I'm sure have taught me more than I've taught them!

Extra special thanks go to the team at Macmillan Education for their support and encouragement and to Phil Woodall, Mark Lester, Lorna Callander, Adrian Bateman, and Richard Storton for sharing their extensive knowledge and great enthusiasm for teaching. A special mention goes to my children, Jake and Holly, for who life is learning and learning is life!

Please see Student's Book imprint page for visual walkthrough photo credits.

The author(s) and publishers are grateful for permission to reprint the following copyright material:

Material from *Critical Thinking Skills 2nd edn 2011* by author Stella Cottrell, copyright © Stella Cottrell 2011, first published by Palgrave Macmillan 2005, reproduced with permission of the publisher.

Printed and bound in Thailand

2018 2017 2016 2015 2014

10 9 8 7 6 5 4 3 2 1

Contents

Map of Student's Book

Unit	Reading text	Reading & critical thinking skills	Language development
UNIT 1 **Gathering** Page 7	Are online "friends" a threat to development? 🇺🇸	Identifying the writer's position What exactly is an argument?	Synonyms Simple and progressive verb forms
UNIT 2 **Games** Page 17	After the Games end: Risks and rewards of hosting the Olympics® 🇬🇧	Identifying contrasts Identifying references to things outside the text	Guessing meaning from context Expressing contrast
UNIT 3 **Nostalgia** Page 27	The shifting sands of memory 🇺🇸	Understanding analogies in a text Identifying sources of information	Reporting information Condensing information with compound adjectives
UNIT 4 **Risk** Page 37	Risk-takers: Who are they? 🇬🇧	Summarizing Assessing whether research supports an argument	Adjective + preposition collocations Infinitive phrases
UNIT 5 **Sprawl** Page 47	Solving the problem of informal settlements 🇬🇧	Identifying different perspectives Recognizing trends and patterns	Prepositional phrases Impersonal report structures
UNIT 6 **Legacy** Page 57	Endangered languages: Strategies for preservation and revitalization 🇺🇸	Using headings to understand the main ideas Identifying fact, speculation, and opinion	Words with more than one affix Relative pronouns with prepositions
UNIT 7 **Expanse** Page 67	Overpopulation: A problem or a myth? 🇺🇸 🇬🇧	Identifying persuasion techniques Assessing the logic of an argument	Adjective + noun collocations Noun (nominal) clauses
UNIT 8 **Change** Page 77	Leadership and change management 🇬🇧	Identifying concepts and theories Inferring criticism	Idiomatic language Participle clauses
UNIT 9 **Flow** Page 87	How rivers made civilisation 🇬🇧	Identifying links Identifying logical fallacies	Verbs and expressions with prepositions Expressing causality
UNIT 10 **Conflict** Page 97	Culture and conflict 🇺🇸	Identifying causes Identifying humor	Phrasal nouns Verb patterns

🇬🇧 = features British English; 🇺🇸 = features American English

Writing skill	Writing task	Digibook video activity	Study skills & Critical thinking skills
Formality	A formal email to a college professor	No man is an island	Study skills: Process writing and peer checking
Creating an outline	A report on hosting a major sports event	Reality TV: The harsh reality	Study skills: Finding an idea to write about
Transition sentences	An essay on the accuracy of memories	Retro-volution	Critical thinking skills: Eyewitness testimony *Stella Cottrell*
Avoiding plagiarism	A summary of a research paper	Risky business	Study skills: Evaluating online sources
Hedging	An argumentative essay	The urban footprint	Critical thinking skills: Internal consistency *Stella Cottrell*
Writing definitions	A comparison essay on endangered languages	Tracing the family line	Study skills: Academic referencing
Emphasizing your point	A persuasive essay about overpopulation	Infinite boundaries	Critical thinking skills: Argument: Persuasion through reasons *Stella Cottrell*
Report writing	A business report for a supermarket	Shock to the system	Study skills: Editing your work
Writing effective conclusions	A cause and effect essay	Volcanic flow	Critical thinking skills: Assuming a causal link *Stella Cottrell*
The writer's voice	An academic essay using an appropriate voice	The warrior gene	Critical thinking skills: Relevant and irrelevant evidence *Stella Cottrell*

Visual walkthrough

VOCABULARY PREVIEW Pre-teaching essential vocabulary which appears in both texts within the unit.

BEFORE YOU READ These introductions to the reading topics prepare students for the upcoming subject matter.

CRITICAL THINKING SKILL Following on from *Global reading*, the *critical thinking skill* sections focus on aspects of texts and provide an in-depth analysis of each text.

Reading skills

Vocabulary preview

1 Match the first half of each definition with the second [illegible]

1 To *rehouse* someone means to
2 *Non-governmental organizations* (NGOs)
3 *Tenancy rights* are
4 *Urbanization* describes
5 A *settlement* is a place where
6 *Infrastructure* describes
7 *Sustainable* resources are
8 A *migrant* is a person who

a the [illegible] city grows because people move there.
b tra[illegible] place or country in order to find work.
c [illegible]ne to a different home.
d [illegible] rights you have to use a piece of land or house.
e [illegible] systems within a place or area, e.g., roads, electricity network.
f people come to live permanently.
g are groups that work with governments in the field of development.
h available for a long time and do not damage the environment.

2 Why are the following important for a growing city? Which is most important?

infrastructure | migrant workers | sustainable resources | tenancy rights

READING Solving the problem of informal settlements

Before you read

Look at the picture below and answer the questions.

1 Why do people live in informal settlements like this? Think of three reasons.
2 What do you think life is like for them? What reasons can you give for this?
3 What name is given to informal settlements like this and the people who live in them in your language? Do you know any other names for them in English?

Global reading

IDENTIFYING DIFFERENT PERSPECTIVES

An analysis of an idea, project, case study, etc. is likely to consider and reference the perspectives of all the groups of people involved, whether this is done explicitly or implicitly. For example, the paper on pages 50–51 looks at informal settlements and includes the viewpoints of various groups involved in those communities.

When reading such a text, it is important to identify the different perspectives to get a much fuller understanding of the issues involved and assess the quality of the analysis. As you read, underline the groups of people that are mentioned and focus on what the writer says about each.

1 Read a paper by Kamal Rajan, a student intern with an NGO, entitled *Solving the problem of informal settlements* on pages 50–51. What is the difference between rehousing people and upgrading settlements?

2 Underline the different groups of people mentioned in the text.

3 Read the paper again and make notes in a table similar to the one below that may reflect each group's perspective on rehousing and upgrading.

	Rehousing	Settlement upgrading
Informal community residents		
Governments		
Other city residents		
NGOs		

48 UNIT 5 SPRAWL

4 Decide whether these occur with the rehousing of residents (*R*), the upgrading of existing communities (*U*), or both (*B*).

1 A more secure home ___
2 Mental well-being ___
3 Greater employment opportunities ___
4 City's infrastructure stretched ___
5 Residents join mainstream society ___
6 Government and community work together ___

Critical thinking skill

RECOGNIZING TRENDS AND PATTERNS

Many academic texts include statistical information. Statistics may describe a static figure, or they may describe a trend or pattern. A trend is a gradual change or development, whereas a pattern is a series of repeated events or actions that tell us how things normally happen.

Over 50% of people live in cities. (= static figure)
Unemployment has risen by 3%. (= trend)
Rent prices have increased to an average of $200 per month. (= trend)
Many families earn just a few dollars each day. (= pattern)
Several hundred people move to the city each month. (= pattern)

When we are not sure about the exact figures, we use vague language with phrases such as *approximately, just over, just under, more than, almost, just, about.*

This number is expected to reach almost 1.5 billion.
Estimated to cost just over $1.2 billion, ...

1 Complete the sentences with a number from the text.

1 There will be ________ people living in cities in 2030, up from ________ in 2008.
2 ________ people live in informal settlements today.
3 ________ more people are expected to move to informal settlements before the end of the decade.
4 ________% of people are estimated to earn less than $30 a month in Kibera.
5 ________% of young people are said to be out of work in Kibera.
6 ________% of jobs are thought to be created by the informal economy.
7 The Mumbai recycling industry has a value of £________.
8 The global population is expected to grow by ________ by 2030.

2 Look at the statistics in exercise 1. Which statistics represent a trend? Which represent a pattern? Which are static figures?

Developing critical thinking

Discuss these questions in a group.

1 What conclusions does the author make? Is he exact about his conclusions or is he vague? How do you know?
2 Do you agree with the author's conclusions? Why or why not?
3 What do you think governments should do to prepare for future migration from rural to urban areas?

SPRAWL UNIT 5 49

Reading skills

GLOBAL READING *Global reading* is the first time the students will read the text; encouraging them to engage with the big issues and the overall picture.

SKILLS BOXES These focus on the newly-presented skill, why it's important, and how to do it. They also highlight reading tips.

DEVELOPING CRITICAL THINKING Developing critical thinking is a chance to reflect on issues presented in the text.

Reading skills

PROJECTS EMAIL SHARE PUBLISH POST TO BLOG

[1] Around 8,000 years ago, new civilisations began to flourish all over the world. In present-day Egypt, China, Iraq, and Pakistan, these groups developed innovations that are the building blocks of human societies today: writing, the wheel, irrigation, trade, laws, and more. The only thing that made all of this possible was water. More specifically, these civilisations arose from rivers: the Nile in Egypt, the Yellow River in China, the Tigris and Euphrates in Mesopotamia, and the Indus in Pakistan. The rivers and their surrounding geography provided people with fertile soil for agriculture, valuable trade routes, and a base for the first real cities. The rivers may even have had an effect on these early peoples' beliefs and worldviews. This essay will examine two significant river valley civilisations—Egypt and Mesopotamia—and the impact of rivers and other aspects of geography on their rise.

Mesopotamia and the Fertile Crescent

[2] Mesopotamia was never a single, unified country; the name comes from a Greek word that means 'land between the rivers' (Wood 2010). In reality, the region was a loose collection of cultures that rose and fell over the millennia, starting around 8,000 years ago, and were often at war with each other (Collon 2011, Wood 2010). They included Sumeria, Assyria, Akkadia, Babylon, and many others (Penn Museum 2012). Despite this disunity, the cultures of Mesopotamia were the first to develop agriculture, domesticate livestock, invent the wheel, build cities, and write literature (Collon 2011).

[3] The rivers of Mesopotamia were the Tigris and the Euphrates, flowing through present-day Iraq and emptying in the Persian Gulf. (They also flowed through parts of Turkey, Syria, and Iran.) In this area, which today we know as the 'fertile crescent', the rivers flooded violently and unpredictably, but the soil left behind by the floods made for excellent farmland for wheat, barley, and dates (Metz 1988). The marshes around the rivers were a source of fish and birds to eat, and reeds growing in the marshes could be used to weave mats and roofs (Penn Museum 2012). These commodities had great value to people around the region. As a result, within a few thousand years, the Mesopotamians had also established trade routes with Iran, India, and the regions to the north. These routes partly made use of the Tigris and Euphrates, but were mostly overland (Penn Museum 2012).

[4] Since the Mesopotamians were organised in large cities, some as large as 100,000 people, there was a labour force large enough to build large-scale irrigation projects. This resulted in more farmland and more food, but also in disputes over land and water (Wood 2010). It is probably not a coincidence that after these conflicts arose, Mesopotamians developed the world's first systems of writing and laws. Without irrigation, they might never have been invented.

90 UNIT 9 FLOW

READING EXCERPTS Interesting and original topics make up the reading excerpts in *Skillful*.

Visual walkthrough

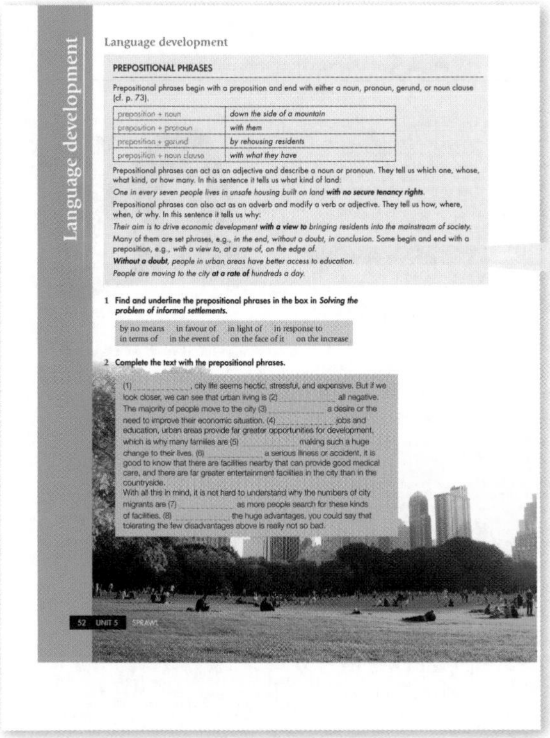

Language development

Language development

PREPOSITIONAL PHRASES

Prepositional phrases begin with a preposition and end with either a noun, pronoun, gerund, or noun clause (cf. p. 73).

preposition + noun	*down the side of a mountain*
preposition + pronoun	*with them*
preposition + gerund	*by rehousing residents*
preposition + noun clause	*with what they have*

Prepositional phrases can act as an adjective and describe a noun or pronoun. They tell us which one, whose, what kind, or how many. In this sentence it tells us what kind of land:

One in every seven people lives in unsafe housing built on land ***with no secure tenancy rights****.*

Prepositional phrases can also act as an adverb and modify a verb or adjective. They tell us how, where, when, or why. In this sentence it tells us why:

Their aim is to drive economic development ***with a view to*** *bringing residents into the mainstream of society.*

Many of them are set phrases, e.g., *in the end, without a doubt, in conclusion.* Some begin and end with a preposition, e.g., *with a view to, at a rate of, on the edge of.*

Without a doubt*, people in urban areas have better access to education.*

People are moving to the city ***at a rate of*** *hundreds a day.*

1 Find and underline the prepositional phrases in the box in *Solving the problem of informal settlements.*

by no means   in favour of   in light of   in response to
in terms of   in the event of   on the face of it   on the increase

2 Complete the text with the prepositional phrases.

(1) ________, city life seems hectic, stressful, and expensive. But if we look closer, we can see that urban living is (2) ________ all negative. The majority of people move to the city (3) ________ a desire or the need to improve their economic situation. (4) ________ jobs and education, urban areas provide far greater opportunities for development, which is why many families are (5) ________ making such a huge change to their lives. (6) ________ a serious illness or accident, it is good to know that there are facilities nearby that can provide good medical care, and there are far greater entertainment facilities in the city than in the countryside.

With all this in mind, it is not hard to understand why the numbers of city migrants are (7) ________ as more people search for these kinds of facilities. (8) ________ the huge advantages, you could say that tolerating the few disadvantages above is really not so bad.

52 UNIT 5 SPRAWL

LANGUAGE DEVELOPMENT Notes on form and function appear in both Student's Books, and provide practice of key points.

SECTION OVERVIEW Giving students the context within which they are going to study the productive skills.

END OF UNIT TASK Comprehensive end-of-unit task with a noticing exercise for students to identify key features.

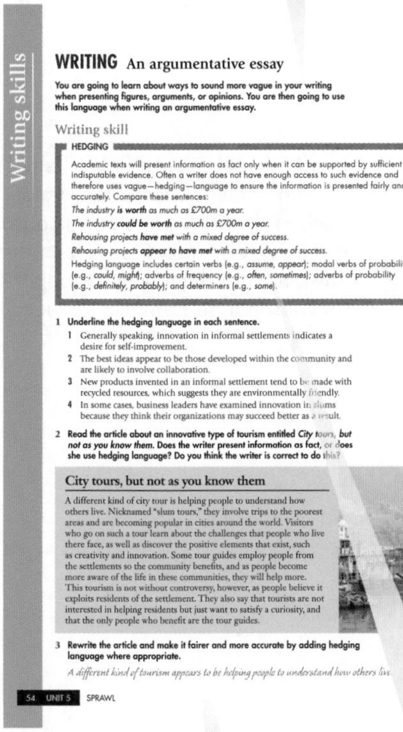

Writing skills

WRITING An argumentative essay

You are going to learn about ways to sound more vague in your writing when presenting figures, arguments, or opinions. You are then going to use this language when writing an argumentative essay.

Writing skill

HEDGING

Academic texts will present information as fact only when it can be supported by sufficient indisputable evidence. Often a writer does not have enough access to such evidence and therefore uses vague—hedging—language to ensure the information is presented fairly and accurately. Compare these sentences:

The industry ***is worth*** *as much as £700m a year.*

The industry ***could be worth*** *as much as £700m a year.*

Rehousing projects ***have met*** *with a mixed degree of success.*

Rehousing projects ***appear to have met*** *with a mixed degree of success.*

Hedging language includes certain verbs (e.g., *assume, appear*); modal verbs of probability (e.g., *could, might*); adverbs of frequency (e.g., *often, sometimes*); adverbs of probability (e.g., *definitely, probably*); and determiners (e.g., *some*).

1 Underline the hedging language in each sentence.

1 Generally speaking, innovation in informal settlements indicates a desire for self-improvement.
2 The best ideas appear to be those developed within the community and are likely to involve collaboration.
3 New products invented in an informal settlement tend to be made with recycled resources, which suggests they are environmentally friendly.
4 In some cases, business leaders have examined innovation in slums because they think their organizations may succeed better as a result.

2 Read the article about an innovative type of tourism entitled *City tours, but not as you know them.* Does the writer present information as fact, or does she use hedging language? Do you think the writer is correct to do this?

City tours, but not as you know them

A different kind of city tour is helping people to understand how others live. Nicknamed "slum tours," they involve trips to the poorest areas and are becoming popular in cities around the world. Visitors who go on such a tour learn about the challenges that people who live there face, as well as discover the positive elements that exist, such as creativity and innovation. Some tour guides employ people from the settlements so the community benefits, and as people become more aware of the life in these communities, they will help more. This tourism is not without controversy, however, as people believe it exploits residents of the settlement. They also say that tourists are not interested in helping residents but just want to satisfy a curiosity, and that the only people who benefit are the tour guides.

3 Rewrite the article and make it fairer and more accurate by adding hedging language where appropriate.

A different kind of tourism appears to be helping people to understand how others live

54 UNIT 5 SPRAWL

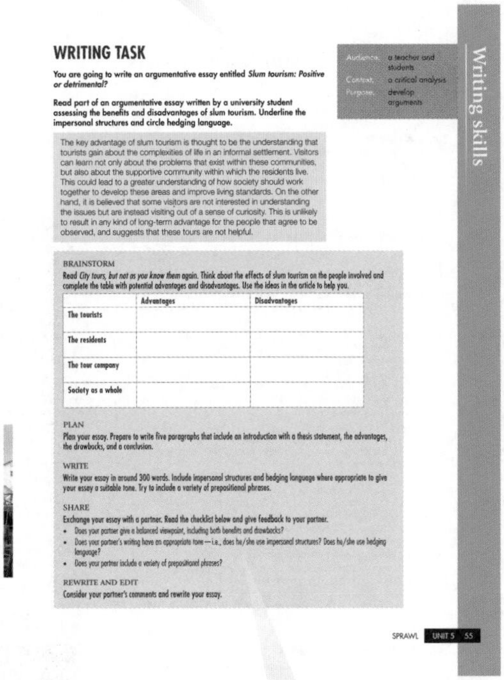

WRITING TASK

You are going to write an argumentative essay entitled *Slum tourism: Positive or detrimental?*

Audience:	a teacher and students
Context:	a critical analysis
Purpose:	develop arguments

Read part of an argumentative essay written by a university student assessing the benefits and disadvantages of slum tourism. Underline the impersonal structures and circle hedging language.

The key advantage of slum tourism is thought to be the understanding that tourists gain about the complexities of life in an informal settlement. Visitors can learn not only about the problems that exist within these communities, but also about the supportive community within which the residents live. This could lead to a greater understanding of how society should work together to develop these areas and improve living standards. On the other hand, it is believed that some visitors are not interested in understanding the issues but are instead visiting out of a sense of curiosity. This is unlikely to result in any kind of long-term advantage for the people that agree to be observed, and suggests that these tours are not helpful.

BRAINSTORM

Read *City tours, but not as you know them* again. Think about the effects of slum tourism on the people involved and complete the table with potential advantages and disadvantages. Use the ideas in the article to help you.

	Advantages	Disadvantages
The tourists		
The residents		
The tour company		
Society as a whole		

PLAN

Plan your essay. Prepare to write five paragraphs that include an introduction with a thesis statement, the advantages, the drawbacks, and a conclusion.

WRITE

Write your essay in around 300 words. Include impersonal structures and hedging language where appropriate to give your essay a suitable tone. Try to include a variety of prepositional phrases.

SHARE

Exchange your essay with a partner. Read the checklist below and give feedback to your partner.

- Does your partner give a balanced viewpoint, including both benefits and drawbacks?
- Does your partner's writing have an appropriate tone—i.e., does he/she use impersonal structures? Does he/she use hedging language?
- Does your partner include a variety of prepositional phrases?

REWRITE AND EDIT

Consider your partner's comments and rewrite your essay.

SPRAWL UNIT 5 55

Writing skills

GUIDED PRACTICE Guides students through the stages of a writing task.

SKILLS BOXES Highlighting writing advice.

WRITING STAGES Gives students support through the stages of the writing process.

CRITICAL THINKING SKILLS WITH STELLA COTTRELL

At the end of each unit, there is either a study skills focus, or a focus on an aspect of critical thinking. The critical thinking pages showcase a theme from Stella Cottrell's bestselling book *Critical Thinking Skills*.

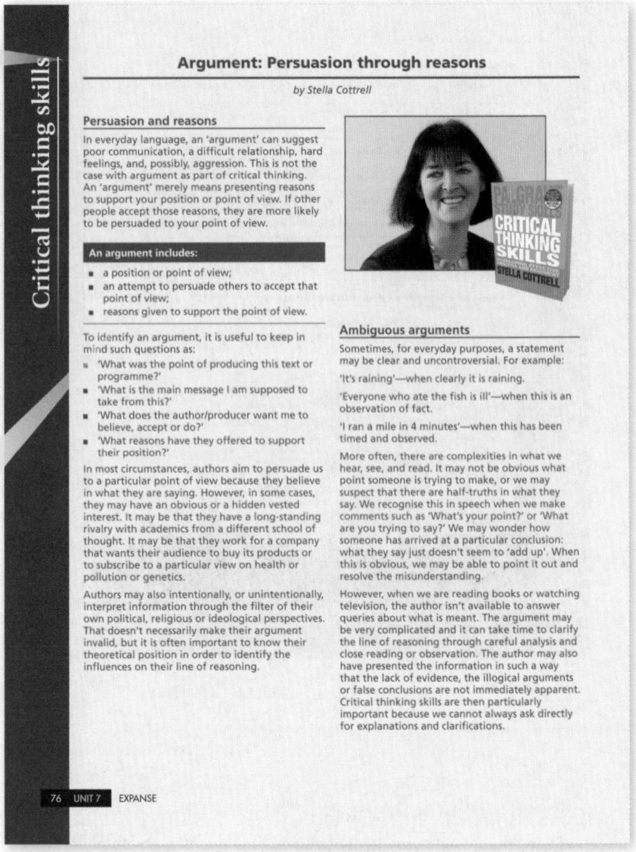

Critical thinking skills

Argument: Persuasion through reasons

by Stella Cottrell

Persuasion and reasons

In everyday language, an 'argument' can suggest poor communication, a difficult relationship, hard feelings, and, possibly, aggression. This is not the case with argument as part of critical thinking. An 'argument' merely means presenting reasons to support your position or point of view. If other people accept those reasons, they are more likely to be persuaded to your point of view.

An argument includes:

- a position or point of view;
- an attempt to persuade others to accept that point of view;
- reasons given to support the point of view.

To identify an argument, it is useful to keep in mind such questions as:

- 'What was the point of producing this text or programme?'
- 'What is the main message I am supposed to take from this?'
- 'What does the author/producer want me to believe, accept or do?'
- 'What reasons have they offered to support their position?'

In most circumstances, authors aim to persuade us to a particular point of view because they believe in what they are saying. However, in some cases, they may have an obvious or a hidden vested interest. It may be that they have a long-standing rivalry with academics from a different school of thought. It may be that they work for a company that wants their audience to buy its products or to subscribe to a particular view on health or pollution or genetics.

Authors may also intentionally, or unintentionally, interpret information through the filter of their own political, religious or ideological perspectives. That doesn't necessarily make their argument invalid, but it is often important to know their theoretical position in order to identify the influences on their line of reasoning.

Ambiguous arguments

Sometimes, for everyday purposes, a statement may be clear and uncontroversial. For example:

'It's raining'—when clearly it is raining.

'Everyone who ate the fish is ill'—when this is an observation of fact.

'I ran a mile in 4 minutes'—when this has been timed and observed.

More often, there are complexities in what we hear, see, and read. It may not be obvious what point someone is trying to make, or we may suspect that there are half-truths in what they say. We recognise this in speech when we make comments such as 'What's your point?' or 'What are you trying to say?' We may wonder how someone has arrived at a particular conclusion: what they say just doesn't seem to 'add up'. When this is obvious, we may be able to point it out and resolve the misunderstanding.

However, when we are reading books or watching television, the author isn't available to answer queries about what is meant. The argument may be very complicated and it can take time to clarify the line of reasoning through careful analysis and close reading or observation. The author may also have presented the information in such a way that the lack of evidence, the illogical arguments or false conclusions are not immediately apparent. Critical thinking skills are then particularly important because we cannot always ask directly for explanations and clarifications.

76 UNIT 7 EXPANSE

EXPLANATION BOXES Provide a clear explanation of what the focus is.

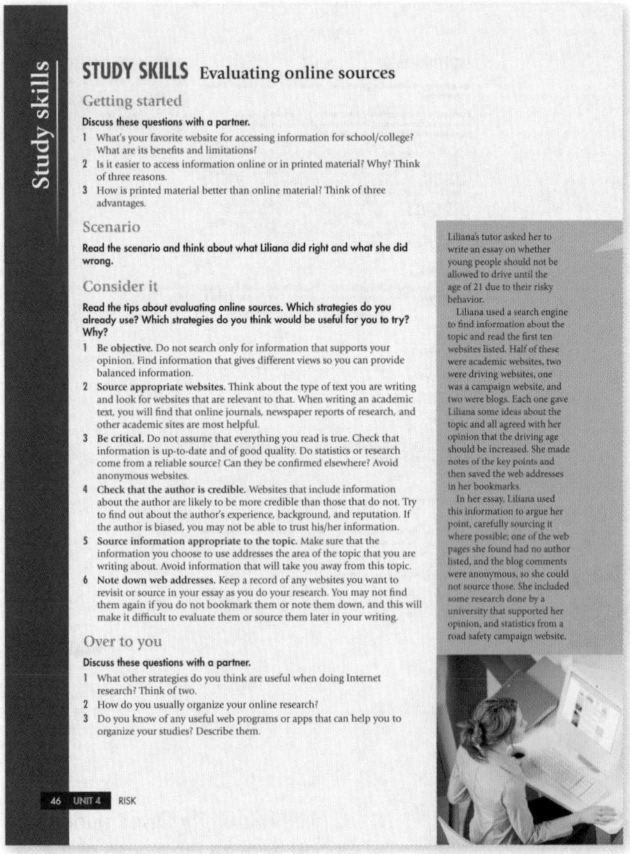

Study skills

STUDY SKILLS Evaluating online sources

Getting started

Discuss these questions with a partner.

1 What's your favorite website for accessing information for school/college? What are its benefits and limitations?
2 Is it easier to access information online or in printed material? Why? Think of three reasons.
3 How is printed material better than online material? Think of three advantages.

Scenario

Read the scenario and think about what Liliana did right and what she did wrong.

Liliana's tutor asked her to write an essay on whether young people should not be allowed to drive until the age of 21 due to their risky behavior.

Liliana used a search engine to find information about the topic and read the first ten websites listed. Half of these were academic websites, two were driving websites, one was a campaign website, and two were blogs. Each one gave Liliana some ideas about the topic and all agreed with her opinion that the driving age should be increased. She made notes of the key points and then saved the web addresses in her bookmarks.

In her essay, Liliana used this information to argue her point, carefully sourcing it where possible; one of the web pages she found had no author listed, and the blog comments were anonymous, so she could not source those. She included some research done by a university that supported her opinion, and statistics from a road safety campaign website.

Consider it

Read the tips about evaluating online sources. Which strategies do you already use? Which strategies do you think would be useful for you to try? Why?

1 **Be objective.** Do not search only for information that supports your opinion. Find information that gives different views so you can provide balanced information.
2 **Source appropriate websites.** Think about the type of text you are writing and look for websites that are relevant to that. When writing an academic text, you will find that online journals, newspaper reports of research, and other academic sites are most helpful.
3 **Be critical.** Do not assume that everything you read is true. Check that information is up-to-date and of good quality. Do statistics or research come from a reliable source? Can they be confirmed elsewhere? Avoid anonymous websites.
4 **Check that the author is credible.** Websites that include information about the author are likely to be more credible than those that do not. Try to find out about the author's experience, background, and reputation. If the author is biased, you may not be able to trust his/her information.
5 **Source information appropriate to the topic.** Make sure that the information you choose to use addresses the area of the topic that you are writing about. Avoid information that will take you away from this topic.
6 **Note down web addresses.** Keep a record of any websites you want to revisit or source in your essay as you do your research. You may not find them again if you do not bookmark them or note them down, and this will make it difficult to evaluate them or source them later in your writing.

Over to you

Discuss these questions with a partner.

1 What other strategies do you think are useful when doing Internet research? Think of two.
2 How do you usually organize your online research?
3 Do you know of any useful web programs or apps that can help you to organize your studies? Describe them.

46 UNIT 4 RISK

STUDY SKILLS SCENARIOS Using original material, the other end-of-unit study skills task gives students a positive or negative scenario to work through. This provides them with the opportunity for personal performance reflection.

SKILLFUL VERSATILITY Both student and teacher facing, the *Skillful* Digibook can be used for group activities in the classroom, on an interactive whiteboard, or by the student alone for homework and extra practice.

DIGIBOOK TOOLBAR The toolbar that appears on each page allows for easy manipulation of the text. Features such as highlighting and a text tool for commenting allow the teacher to add points as the class goes along, and functions like the zoom and grab tool mean the teacher can focus students' attention on the appropriate sections.

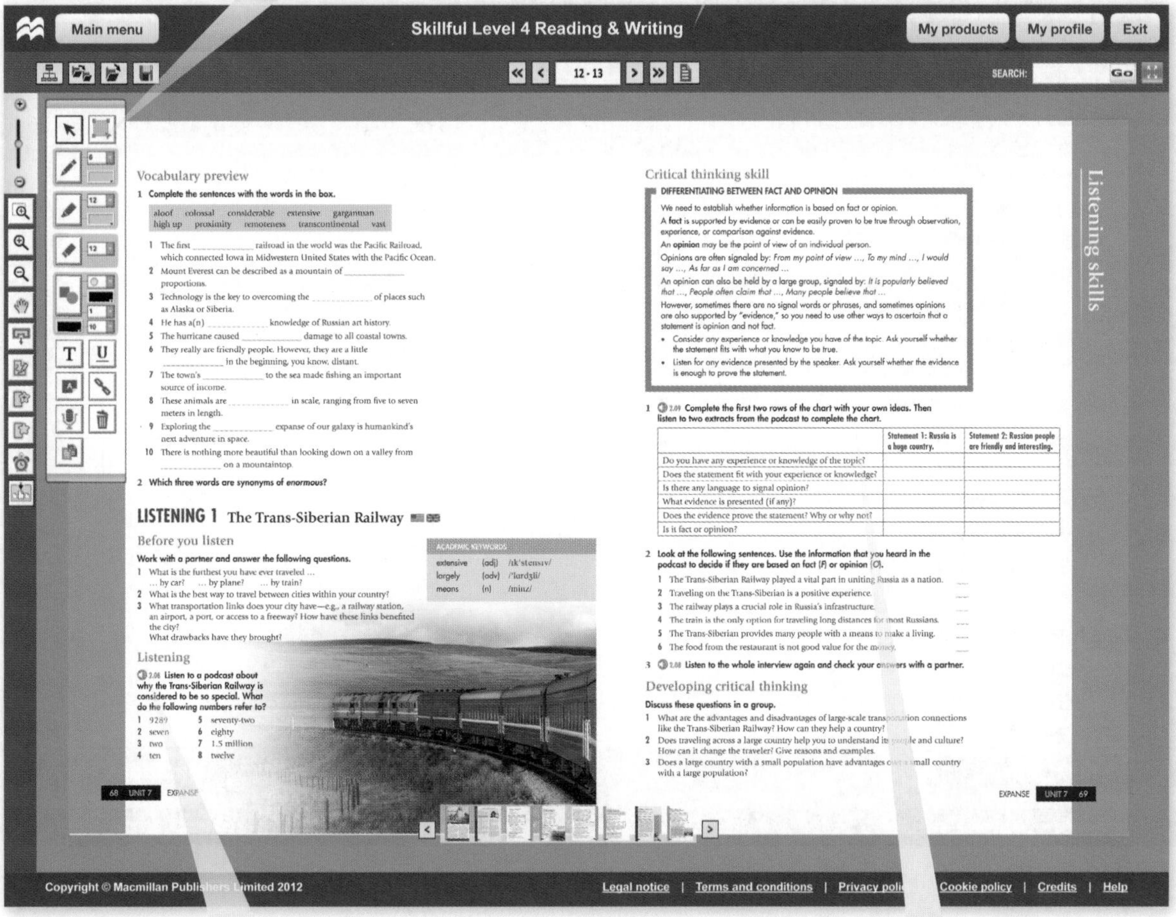

EMBEDDED AUDIO For instant access to the audio for unit exercises, the Digibook has embedded files that you can reach in one click.

PAGE-FAITHFUL Provides a digital replica of the *Skillful* Student's Books while hosting additional, interactive features.

WHAT IS *SKILLFUL* PRACTICE? The *Skillful* practice area is a student-facing environment designed to encourage extra preparation, and provides additional activities for listening, vocabulary, grammar, speaking, and pronunciation as well as support videos for listening and alternative unit assignments.

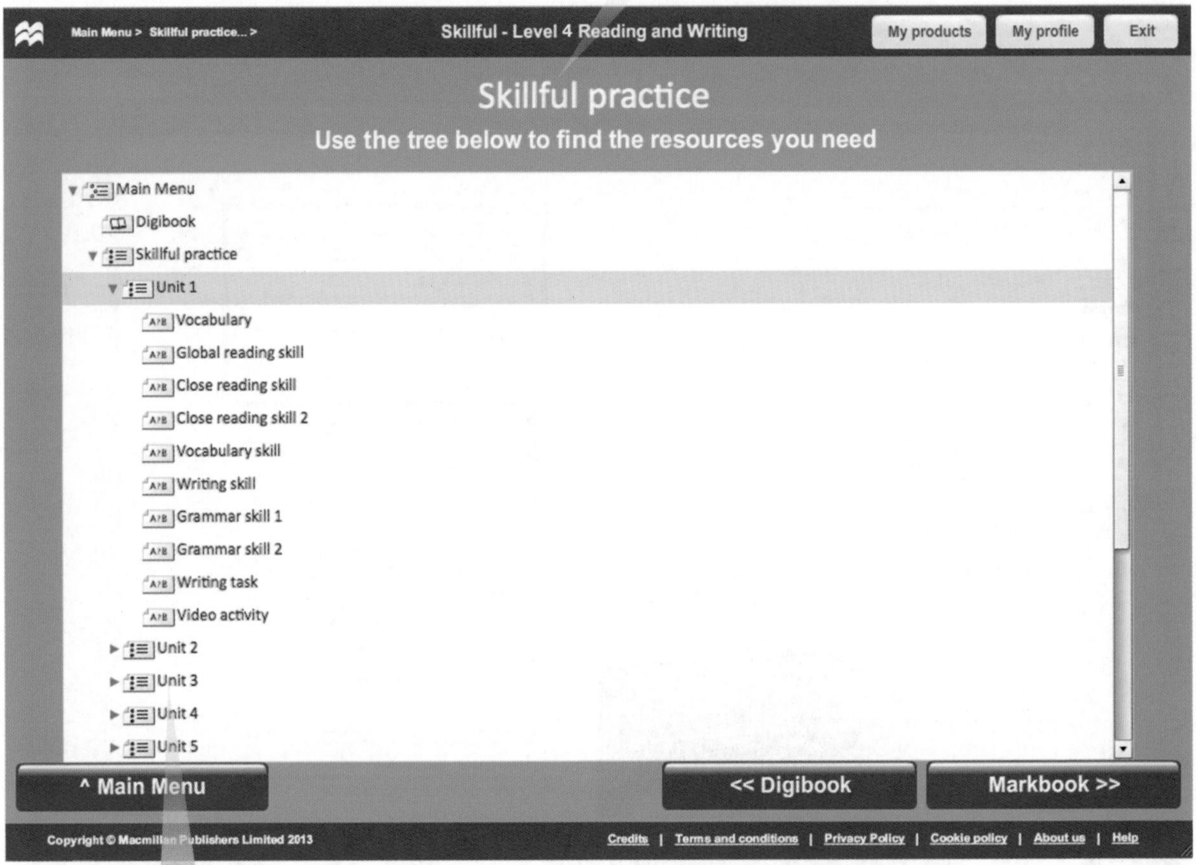

UNIT AND TASK SELECTION
Handy drop-down menus allow students to jump straight to their practice unit and the exercise they want to concentrate on.

TEACHER RESOURCES The *Skillful* teachers have many more resources at their fingertips.

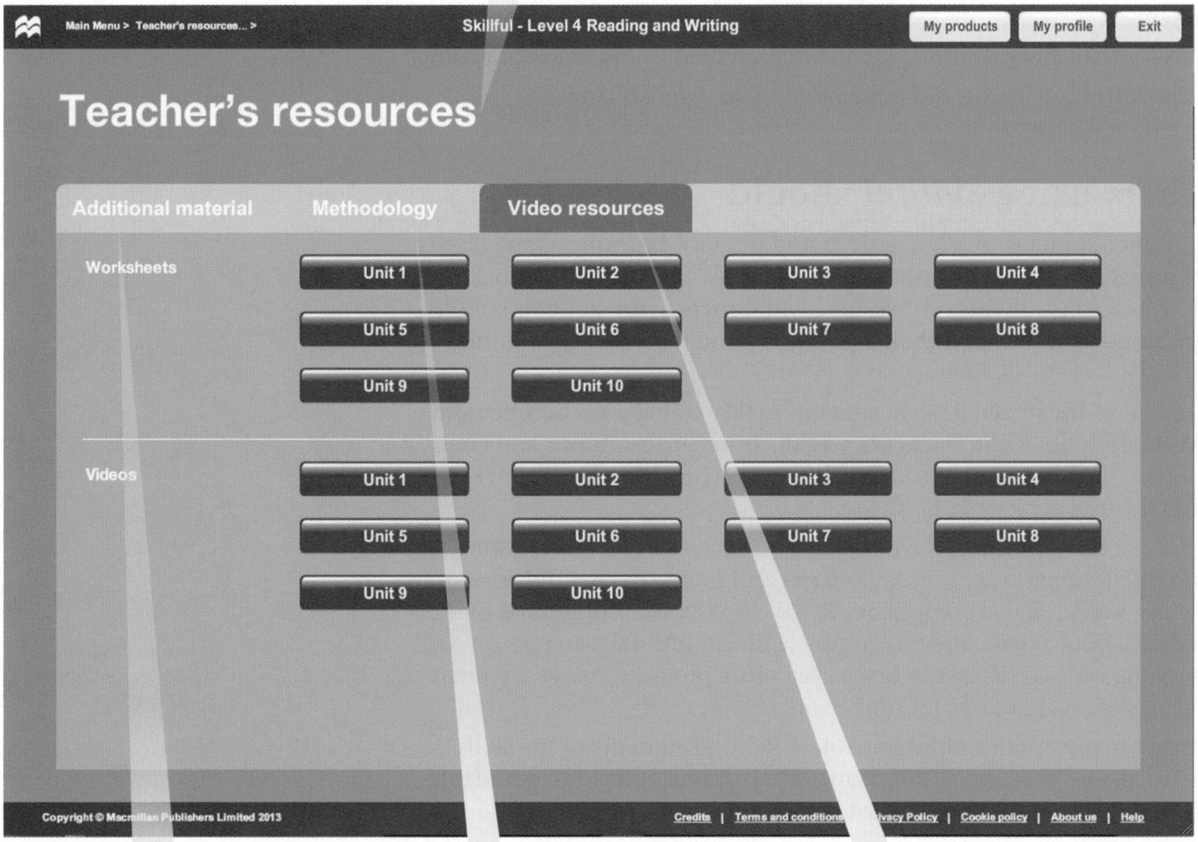

ADDITIONAL MATERIAL Along with the student add-ons there are printable worksheets, test materials, and a markbook component to grade and monitor student progress.

METHODOLOGY For teachers who may need a little extra help to effectively utilize all of the resources *Skillful* has to offer, there are course methodology notes.

VIDEO RESOURCES Teachers have access to the same videos as the students, and to complement these there are printable video worksheets to aid lesson planning.

To the teacher

Academic success requires so much more than memorizing facts. It takes skills. This means that a successful student can both learn and think critically. *Skillful* helps teachers prepare their students for academic work in English by teaching not only language—vocabulary and grammar—but the necessary skills to engage with topics, texts, and discourse with classmates.

Skillful gives students

- engaging texts on a wide variety of topics, each examined from two different academic disciplines
- skills for learning about a wide variety of topics from different angles and from different academic areas
- skills they need to succeed when reading and listening to these texts
- skills they need to succeed when writing for and speaking to different audiences
- skills for critically examining the issues presented by a speaker or a writer
- study skills for learning and remembering the English language and important information.

Teachers using *Skillful* should:

- Encourage students to ask questions and interact. Learning a language is not passive. Many of the tasks and exercises involve pairwork, groupwork, and whole-class discussion. Working with others helps students solidify their understanding, and challenge and expand their ability to think critically.
- Personalize the material. Help students make connections between the texts in their book and their own world—home, community, and country. Bring in outside material from local sources when it's relevant, making sure it fits the unit topics and language.
- Provide a lot of practice. Have students do each exercise several times, with different partners. Review exercises and material from previous units. Use the *Skillful* digital component to develop the skills presented in the Student's Book. Have students complete the additional activities on a computer outside of class to make even more progress. Assign frequent manageable review tasks for homework.
- Provide many opportunities for review. Remind students of the skills, grammar, and vocabulary they learned in previous units. Have students study a little bit each day, not just before tests.
- Show students how to be independent learners. Point out opportunities to study and practice English outside of class, such as reading for pleasure and using the Internet in English. Have them find and share information about the different unit topics with the class. The *Study skills* section in every unit gives students valuable tips for successfully managing their own learning.

Learning skills, like learning a language, takes time and practice. Students must be patient with themselves as they put in the necessary time and effort. They should set and check goals. Periodic assessments the teacher can print, such as the unit tests, progress tests, and end test on the digital component let students see their own progress and measure how much they've learned, so they can feel proud of their academic and linguistic development.

The *Skillful* blend by Dorothy E. Zemach

In some academic disciplines, students can begin by acquiring a lot of facts and general knowledge. In a language, however, students need far more than information—they need skills. They need to know how to do things: how to explain, persuade, ask for help, extend an invitation, outline and argue a thesis, distinguish between important and unimportant information, follow digressions, understand implied information, and more.

Skillful recognizes that skills such as these can't be learned by memorizing facts. To acquire these skills, students must notice them as they read or listen; break them down and understand them through clear explanations; and then rehearse and apply those skills in carefully scaffolded activities that lead to freer practice.

The listening and reading texts in each unit introduce students to one subject area explored through two different academic disciplines and two distinct genres. Students learn and practice both global skills, such as recognizing tone and identifying the main idea, and close skills, such as understanding pronoun references and figuring out vocabulary from context, to understand the texts on several levels.

These days, students must interact with both digital and printed text, online and offline, in the classroom and in the workplace. The *Skillful* textbooks are therefore supplemented with the *Skillful* digital components. These further develop, explain, and extend the skills work found in the printed textbooks. They provide additional exercises related to the skills, the grammar points, and the vocabulary areas. They can be accessed either via the Digibook or through the *Skillful* practice area. Scores are tracked and recorded, and if students work offline, their markbook will be updated the next time they connect to the Internet.

Videos for each unit provide additional subject area content that review the skills and language taught in the unit. The videos can be shown in class to feed in additional content, and the accompanying worksheets can be used to structure the lesson.

Unit checklists help students keep track of language in the unit and review for tests.

The digital components also help teachers with classroom organization and management by assigning and tracking homework, and monitoring student progress using the markbook. A full suite of test materials can be used for placement into the appropriate level, and then provide end-of-unit tests and end-of-course tests that can be used as both formative assessments (to evaluate progress) and summative assessments (to mark achievements and assign grades). Tests are provided in both editable and non-editable formats enabling teachers to manipulate the content, as desired. The format of these tests is similar to internationally recognized standardized tests.

Dorothy E. Zemach taught ESL for over 18 years, in Asia, Africa, and the U.S. She holds an MA in TESL, and now concentrates on writing and editing ELT materials and conducting teacher training workshops. Her areas of specialty and interest are teaching writing, teaching reading, business English, academic English, and testing.

Teaching study skills by Stella Cottrell

There is a growing awareness that students' performance, even in higher education, can be improved through training in relevant academic skills.

Hurley (1994) described study skills as "key skills for all areas of education, including advanced study" and argued that students benefit when these skills are taught explicitly. In other words, it should not be assumed that the skills a student brings from school, or even from the first year of university, are sufficient to carry them through their degree. Skills such as task management, working with others, and critical thinking need to be fine-tuned and extended as students move from one level to another.

Globally, universities and colleges are giving far more attention to preparatory support for prospective students and to developing study skills once a student is on a program. In some countries, there is a growing emphasis, too, on "employability skills," from soft skills such as communication, creativity, and working collaboratively to new attributes sought by employers, including business acumen, cross-cultural sensitivity, and enterprise. In addition, each institution tends to identify a range of skills and qualities that it wants to see embodied by its graduates.

One of the challenges is articulating what is meant by study skills in this changing environment. This has significance for students when trying to make sense of long lists of skills that they are expected to accumulate during their time in higher education. It also has a bearing on who teaches and supports study skills. In some colleges and universities, this falls to study skills specialists; in others, it may be allocated to teaching staff. In each case, different approaches are used to make sense of the learning experience.

From the students' perspective, it helps to organize study skills into a few, relatively easy-to-remember categories. In the latest version of *The Study Skills Handbook*, I suggest using four basic categories:

1 Self 2 Academic 3 People 4 Task

The starting place for students is being able to manage themselves within a new learning environment with confidence and resilience. They need to understand the rationale for, and benefits of, independent study and the kinds of challenges that they will be set. This involves organizing their time, coping with deadlines, and recognizing what it means to take charge of their own learning. It also includes metacognitive skills in reflecting on how they think, learn, and manage themselves for study.

Academic skills consist of such skills as the core research skills (finding, recording, and using information); thinking skills (critical thinking skills, creative problem-solving, and synthesis); understanding academic conventions (the nature and integrity of academic study); and writing skills.

People skills are increasingly important as collaborative study becomes a feature of higher education. These include such skills as giving and receiving criticism, supporting others without cheating, group project work, and playing an active role in group sessions. These can be an especial challenge for international students who may be used to different kinds of learning interactions.

Task management skills within this learning context include such skills as meeting given requirements, and using appropriate protocols and project management in order to achieve a given academic task such as writing an essay or report, undertaking research, conducting an experiment, or solving a problem.

An additional value of this framework is that the basic shell can be easily adapted to other contexts, such as employability. The "Self / People / Tasks" model is one that I used, for example, within *Skills for Success: Personal Development and Employability* (2010).

Stella Cottrell is Director for Lifelong Learning at the University of Leeds, U.K. She is author of the bestselling *The Study Skills Handbook, The Palgrave Student Planner, The Exam Skills Handbook, Critical Thinking Skills, Study Skills Connected,* and *Skills for Success,* all published by Palgrave Macmillan.

Reference

Hurley, J. (1994), *Supporting Learning* (Bristol: The Staff College and Learning Partners).

Teaching academic vocabulary by Pete Sharma

It has been estimated that in an academic text, a quarter of the words are either "academic vocabulary" or "technical vocabulary." What is "academic vocabulary"? The term includes:

- concepts, such as *research*
- actions, such as *classifying* and *defining*
- nouns, such as *sources* and *references*
- collocations, such as *reading list*, and
- reporting language, such as *argue*.

Academic vocabulary is used across all disciplines. This essay will describe a range of activities for teaching academic vocabulary.

Students meet and practice new vocabulary in every kind of lesson, and especially in reading and listening lessons. In a listening lesson, you may pre-teach key vocabulary before students do the listening task. Similarly, in a reading lesson, you can pre-teach specific words to make the text easier to read. Throughout the *Skillful* Students' Book, there are "Vocabulary skill" boxes, as well as "Academic keyword" boxes which signal important words.

Giving presentations provides opportunities for students to use and practice new vocabulary, and for you to provide feedback on their pronunciation. Similarly, writing essays allows learners to produce the new words they have learned in context.

During the course, you will not only present and practice vocabulary, but also give advice on effective learning strategies. Explore the different ways students can record the new vocabulary they meet on the course. Many students merely jot down a word and write a translation next to it, so it is helpful to present alternatives, such as creating "word trees." Have students work together to create mind-maps on relevant topics, as we remember words when we meet them in concept groups. The *Skillful* Teacher's Book includes several ideas for using a vocabulary notebook. Point out that many words have a standard meaning and an academic meaning. Give examples: *references; argument.*

Students frequently start their academic course over-using their bilingual dictionary. They benefit from a lesson or lessons exploring the pros and cons of using a monolingual, English–English dictionary. A good way to start a dictionary lesson is to do a quiz to show some useful dictionary features in the dictionary. Part of a lesson can be spent introducing learners to electronic dictionaries, which allow students to listen to new words. You can demonstrate a CD-ROM and web-based dictionary using a data projector.

There are several important features of academic vocabulary that you will wish to focus on during the course. It is useful to provide practice on prefixes and suffixes, since noticing patterns in the language can help learners work out the meaning of new words. Also, focus on "collocation" or "word partnerships."

Before students read a text, you can select some key collocations, write them on cards, and get students to match them. Students can then scan the text and highlight these collocations before moving to more intensive reading practice.

There are several language exercises on prefixes, suffixes, and collocations in *Skillful* and the Teacher's Book also contains sets of photocopiable cards which can be used in many ways, as warmers, for example, or for reviewing lexis.

There is no need to develop a new methodology for teaching academic vocabulary. Good practice involves students meeting new words in context, practicing them in speaking and writing, and recycling them in a variety of ways. Working through the units and different levels of *Skillful* will enable students to practice and review academic vocabulary systematically.

Pete Sharma is an associate lecturer at Oxford Brookes University, U.K. He has written books on technology in language teaching, and is co-author of *Blended Learning* (Macmillan: 2007) and *400 Ideas for Interactive Whiteboards* (Macmillan: 2010).

Teaching academic reading and writing skills with digital media by Craig Stevens

The demands of modern higher education require both excellent reading and writing skills. Listening and speaking skills are also important in terms of learning from lectures, seminar discussions and presentations, but almost all courses require continuous assessment in terms of written coursework with a final research dissertation and written examinations. Thus, the majority of assessed work at university is heavily dependent upon reading and writing skills.

Can these two key skills be taught effectively by adapting the digital tools and resources that are commonplace in many of our students' lives today? The internet, the interactive whiteboard, the smartphone, and tablet as well as their associated applications (apps) means that there are numerous electronic media options available to learners and teachers inside and outside the classroom. Recent developments in English for Academic Purposes (EAP) has resulted in more resources available, which can be particularly appealing to today's student. Moreover, these resources are presented in formats for smartphones and tablets carried by most students.

College can be a very daunting prospect, particularly if studying in a second language. It is essential that students master effective and efficient reading skills before embarking on a course in order to optimize their study time. Encouraging students to engage and communicate with their peers online can help them practice many of these skills. For example, social bookmarking enables users to share, edit, and annotate bookmarks of web documents with EAP relevance such as scholarly articles. Students can also participate in online discussion boards and other recommended sites for language development. By using tagging, users can organize these bookmarks in multiple ways and develop shared vocabularies. Such activity develops the ability to skim and scan for relevance and facts to locate useful models of writing to analyze. Data capture tools can be used to capture and organize academic documents and papers for extensive reading and further practice of reading strategies. Texts are also available as e-books for portability.

Effective mastery of writing skills includes not only excellent note-taking skills during lectures, but also the ability to produce different types of essays. Students also have to master the ability of writing under time pressure during examinations.

Audio/video software and real-time voice communication tools allow real-time note-taking opportunities. Online discussion boards and online seminars also provide writing practice. Podcasts can be written and recorded by students for course input requiring note-taking and can form the basis of written work. For research project practice, online questionnaires can be used to provide data for discussion and presentation and incorporation into written work. Written work can be uploaded to file-sharing sites for peer review and evaluation. Plagiarism-checking services can aid students in practicing paraphrasing and rephrasing/synthesis skills. Tutoring is also possible to formally practice writing skills.

Overall, digital resources can easily be adapted for the teaching of academic reading and writing skills. These resources offer not only user-friendliness, and convenience, but also the ability to target sub-skills to foster marked improvements in academic reading and writing ability. *Skillful's* digital resources have been designed with this in mind.

Craig Stevens holds an MA in TEFL/Linguistics and has been teaching EFL, ESOL, and EAP for the past 18 years. He is currently teaching EAP at the University of Bristol and the University of the West of England's International College. Craig is a Trinity International ESOL examiner and independent education consultant. His specialist areas include academic reading and writing skills, IT skills, testing spoken English, and English for aviation.

Integrating reading and writing skills by David Bohlke

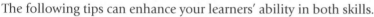

The connection between reading and writing may seem obvious. Both use the written form, but their connection goes much deeper than that. Today, these two skills are still at times taught separately, but it is actually difficult to separate them.

What do we do when we read and write? Writing is an active process. There is no writing unless we create it. Reading, however, has traditionally been seen as more passive. But this view is changing. Deriving meaning from reading relies on the interaction between the writer, text, and reader. This, along with context, determines what a particular text may mean to any particular reader. Reading can be used to improve performance on a writing task. To appreciate good writing, it is important for learners to see how language works in different ways. A reading can also provide new, inspiring ideas for a writing assignment. This exposure to authentic language in a natural context is highly beneficial to writers. The text can also act as a model for a specific writing genre showing correct register, organization structure, and tone. Writing can be used to better understand reading. When we read, actions such as highlighting, taking notes, or writing summaries encourage readers to be more active. By making the comprehension of the text more "visible," this may help the reader remember key points. It also shows that the author's voice is not necessarily the last word on the subject.

The following tips can enhance your learners' ability in both skills.

1 **Draw on what you know** Good readers activate background knowledge when they engage with a text. By tapping into this, they make important connections to the new information encountered in a text. Good writers also activate prior knowledge through brainstorming activities.

2 **Vary your sentences** Good readers know good writing when they see it. They are constantly applying their knowledge of grammar to build comprehension of a text. Good writers also use a variety of sentence patterns to engage and entertain the reader.

3 **Build vocabulary** Good readers build vocabulary through continued reading. Possessing a rich vocabulary allows readers to read with less effort and with a deeper understanding. Good writers use clear, precise words to state exactly what they mean, and are competent users of both a dictionary and a thesaurus.

4 **Understand coherence** Coherence is the unity created among the various ideas, sentences, and paragraphs of a text. Good readers can recognize a coherent text through the author's use of transition words, parallel structure, and sense of organization. Good writers stay on topic and do not offer irrelevant details that distract or confuse the reader.

5 **Identify your audience** Good readers feel a connection with the text, and by extension, its writer. They often imagine the writer is speaking directly to them. Good writers always consider their audience. They anticipate the readers' response and carry on an internal dialogue with them as they write.

6 **Know your genres** Each genre has its own unique characteristics, style, and purpose. Good readers use this knowledge to help them identify text type, predict content, follow an argument, and draw conclusions. Good writers are familiar with different genres and use knowledge of their structural characteristics to produce appropriate texts.

7 **Develop critical thinking** Good readers do not just decode a text and take away its literal meaning. They understand what a text means, rather than just what it says or does. This involves considering, analyzing, evaluating, and inferring to find a deeper understanding of a text. Good critical writers are also good critical readers. They assess and interpret key information and draw conclusions from them.

Connecting reading and writing in the classroom is an important step toward reinforcing learning in both skill areas. Because academic success depends on interacting with a text in multiple ways, development in both is essential.

David Bohlke has 25 years of experience as a teacher, trainer, program director, editor, and materials developer. He has taught in Japan, South Korea, Saudi Arabia, and Morocco, and has conducted multiple teacher-training workshops around the world.

UNIT 1 GATHERING

Reading	Identifying the writer's position
Critical thinking	What exactly is an argument?
Language development	Synonyms Simple and progressive verb forms
Writing	Formality

As this is the first lesson, it is worth spending some time making sure that students feel relaxed and comfortable. Ask students to look at the picture and say what they think it portrays. Ask questions to stimulate ideas: *Where do you think this picture was taken? What can you see in the picture? Have you ever been in a place like this? How do you think the picture is related to the unit title, Gathering?* etc.

Background information

The picture probably shows a technology trade fair or online gaming event in Germany. (This is suggested by some of the signage on the wall.) The people have gathered because they share an interest in computing technology. There are camp beds and food, so the participants are probably attending for a while.

Remember that at any stage the students can access the *Skillful* digital component through the access codes in their Student's Books. Teachers can also access extra items such as tests through the access codes in the Teacher's Book. The activities in the digital component don't have to be done in a fixed order. In the digital component, both students and teachers can also find the Digibook. This is a page-faithful representation of the Student's Book. It could be projected on to a screen such as an interactive whiteboard.

Discussion point

Start with a quick brainstorm of social networking sites students know about or use (e.g., Facebook, Twitter, Kik Messenger, mixi, netlog, etc.). Write these on the board. Ask students what their definition of social networking is. Find out what other ways students have of social networking (such as joining after school clubs), before asking them to discuss the questions with a partner. Examples of other ways to network include meeting friends in cafes, attending events together, and chatting outside of class. If the class is small enough, question 1 could be done as a class poll. For questions 2 and 3, students should discuss in pairs or groups of three. Monitor students' conversations, encouraging them to give reasons for their answers. In the feedback session, ask students to share some of the ideas from their discussion. Demonstrate seminar-type discussion by asking students to speak and respond to each other, not just the teacher.

Cultural awareness

Different countries have different social networking sites. Netlog is popular in the Middle East, mixi is Japanese, and renren is Chinese. These sites are similar to Facebook, but are not all in English.

As part of the routine for the beginning of each unit, it is a good idea to refer students to the box which shows the learning objectives. Knowing the objectives helps students understand why they are doing certain tasks and what they should aim to learn from them. Ask students to read the objectives box on page 7. At the end of the unit, refer students to the box again.

Vocabulary preview

Students at this level should be encouraged to decipher the meaning of unknown words from context when possible and to use a good monolingual dictionary if needed.

Find out how students keep track of and learn new vocabulary. They should develop a system using a notebook or notecards. Show students, with an example word (perhaps the unit title, *Gathering*), how they can note important information about each word: the definition(s), part of speech, word forms, collocations, stress patterns, and example sentences which contextualize the term. A brief translation into the students' mother tongues can be helpful, although students should not rely on this. Many words have more than one meaning, so context is key to understanding the meaning, nuance, and usage.

1 Ask students to work in pairs to read the sentences and match the underlined words to the meanings in the box. Tell them not to use translators or dictionaries, but to rely on the context to help them. When going over the answers, ask students what clues they used to figure out the correct definitions.

ANSWERS

1 people you know
2 evidence based on observation
3 different
4 develops
5 someone who is interested only in him/herself
6 connections
7 children who are changing into young adults
8 help to develop
9 always linked to people via technology
10 ability to understand how someone feels

EXTENSION ACTIVITY

A wiki is a website which allows its readers to freely add and edit content, and create links between different pieces of content. Start a class wiki to provide a tailored, online study guide for the vocabulary in the book. Divide the class into ten groups. Each group will be in charge of setting up wiki entries for the vocabulary from one unit. First, set up a class wiki (search for *set up class wiki* to find out how, or use *wikispaces.com*). Next, ask students what kinds of information they think would be useful to post (e.g., word forms charts, definitions, example sentences, collocations). Set the input task for homework, and remind the group to add new vocabulary as it comes up within the unit. Remind the rest of the class to visit the wiki as part of their studying during the unit.

This is a good point to introduce the students to the digital component activities. These additional activities support the sections covered in the Student's Book and provide extra practice for students either at home or in the classroom.

READING Are online "friends" a threat to development?

Word count 1,028

Background information

Online social networking continues to grow. According to Facebook's 2013 report, 1.11 billion people use the site.

A list of other networks shows users in the millions.

Social networking via computing technology has actually been around since the 70s. Computer hobbyists and technophiles communicated via services such as BBS and CompuServe. However, it was really only with the growth of the Internet that social networking sites started their big growth. Some of the earliest sites included Classmates.com and SixDegrees.com. Niche sites included AsianAvenue.com, BlackPlanet.com, and MiGente.com. Then came Friendster, LinkedIn, MySpace, Facebook, and Twitter. Wikipedia has a list of 200 of the most active social networking sites which it says is far from comprehensive.

So, what does the future of social networking look like? Younger users are already abandoning Facebook for sites that their parents aren't on and sites that allow more open access with no advertising. More and more users are uploading their own apps, too, so sharing is becoming even bigger. It appears that people today are adapting social networking to better suit modern purposes.

Before you read

Write the title of the reading text on the board. Ask students why they think the word *friends* is in quotation marks. (The quotation marks indicate that the friends people have online may not be true friends.) Ask them to predict briefly what the article might include, then put them into pairs to discuss the questions. You may need to pre-teach the verb *outweigh*. In this context, it means that the advantages are more important or more valuable than the disadvantages. In the feedback session, note the advantages and disadvantages on the board for question 1, and ask students to give reasons to support their views for question 2.

Global reading

1 Ask students to read the question and think about the areas of impact the author may mention for one minute. Brainstorm ideas on the board.

2 Give students four minutes to skim the text on pages 10–11 to see if the ideas on the board are mentioned. They should not use dictionaries at this point because the main aim is to read quickly to check their ideas. As students read, watch them to see what they do when they read. Some students may use their finger as they read, others may spend a long time on one sentence. Poor readers will get stuck on unknown words, whereas good readers will skip unknown words and try to figure out the meaning from context. Depending on your group, you may need to review good reading strategies. After students have finished reading, discuss which of the ideas on the board from the *Before you read* section were mentioned.

This would be a good time to draw students' attention to the *Academic keywords* box on page 11. Academic keywords are terms that occur frequently in academic texts, so they are particularly important for those students who plan to study in English in higher education. The Digibook features the same academic keywords, but with definitions. If you have set up wiki groups, they should add the keywords in this unit to the wiki.

SUPPORTING CRITICAL THINKING

Identifying the writer's position is an important critical thinking skill, especially at advanced levels. It is important to recognize when a writer agrees or disagrees with the views he/she presents because it is in this way the reader can judge the arguments of the writer. Writers may use adjectives, adverbs, opinion language, and linking phrases to direct the reader and build their argument, though in many academic texts, writers may rely less on adjectives and adverbs and more on linking phrases. Recognizing how a writer builds an argument is also important as students begin to portray their position in their own writing.

As a lead-in, write *identifying the writer's position* on the board. Ask students what they think *position* means in this context. Refer them to the *Identifying the writer's position* box and give them a couple of minutes to read it. Has their idea of what *position* means changed? Why do they think it is important to be able to identify the writer's view?

3 Refer students to exercise 3 and give them a few minutes to discuss the questions in pairs.

ANSWERS
Writer's position = 2, 4

Critical thinking skill

Students may know the term *argument* in the context of a disagreement, but in this context it has a different meaning. Ask students to read the *What exactly is an argument?* box to find out what it means in this context. Check that they have understood that in the academic definition, an argument has nothing to do with disagreement. Find out if they think giving reasons for opinions is important when trying to make a point.

Cultural awareness

Generally at Western universities, students are expected to give reasons for their opinions and to formulate logical arguments based on evidence. It is not about disrespecting other people's ideas, particularly from senior professors, but a chance to demonstrate a student's depth of thinking and academic ability. Much of the evidence used in an academic argument comes from other scholars and authors. Students have to show their ability to build a good argument both in writing and in seminar discussions.

1 Ask students to read the text again and do exercise 1. Encourage students to read quickly. They may wish to highlight unknown words to look up later at home. Early finishers can compare and discuss their answers. Then feed back on answers.

ANSWERS

1 The impact of technology on the nature of our friendships has been a much-debated topic since the meteoric rise of social networks.
2 In fact there is a lot of research that shows these criticisms are generally unfounded.
3 They also found that social networks allow us to have discussions with a much more diverse set of people than in the real world, so we share knowledge with people from a wide variety of backgrounds.
4 A study conducted by Michigan State University (2010) concluded that our virtual friendships provide social benefits and improve our psychological well-being.
5 Research is starting to show that this culture is negatively affecting not our friendships but our character.
6 Through her years of research, she has noticed that these devices permit us to have complete control over our friendships.
7 Friendships are unpredictable and difficult to deal with, but social networks are allowing people to tidy them up and manage them.
8 Turkle also suggests that people are no longer comfortable being alone.

2 Ask students to do exercise 2 and then compare their answers in pairs.

ANSWERS
1 d **2** a **3** a **4** f **5** c **6** d **7** e **8** b & e

3 For this exercise, students should identify the points which are not arguments, using the definition of *argument* they learned earlier. They should be prepared to give reasons for their choices.

ANSWER
1 and 6 are not arguments because the statements are not supported by evidence/reasons.

Developing critical thinking

Background information
The aim of this section is for students to discuss their ideas and opinions in groups, so it is important to encourage all students to speak. In this context, *critical* means *reflective, analytical, or evaluative thinking* and has nothing to do with being negative. Some students may not be used to this kind of task, so you may need to tell them the aim and how it will benefit them.

Before beginning the task, make sure students understand the definition of *critical thinking*. Explain that this is the ability to reflect on the quality of beliefs and opinions, and should not be confused with the negative sense of criticism. Showing that they are thinking critically includes giving reasons for their opinions and putting forth a good argument.

Ask students to think about how they perform in a group discussion. Do they talk a lot? Do they ask others questions? Refer them to the functional language on page 108 of the Student's Book and ask them to identify one functional area they would like to be better at. They should choose a phrase from that area that they would like to use during the discussion which follows.

Put students into groups of three or four for the discussion task. Monitor discussions to encourage all students to speak.

EXTENSION ACTIVITY

Ask students to find and highlight the vocabulary from page 8 in the text. They should note the word form, how the word is used in context, and any collocations that they find, e.g., the collocation *narcissistic tendencies* in paragraph 8.

Language development: Synonyms

Cultural awareness

In some cultures, using the same word repetitively in the same paper is considered poor writing. While the word *friend* or *friendship* does appear 18 times in the reading on pages 10–11, synonym use is generally preferred. Writers need to choose synonyms with the same meaning and level of formality: in the example given in the *Synonyms* box, *spend time* is slightly more formal than *hang out; hang out* is too informal for an academic piece of writing. A good monolingual dictionary will have notes about levels of formality. A thesaurus is useful for finding synonyms.

Ensure students know what a synonym is and ask them to scan paragraph 3 on page 10 to find a synonym for *friends* (*companions*). Ask students why writers use synonyms and how important they think they are. Ask them to read the *Synonyms* box to find out three important points to remember about synonyms (some mean the same thing, some have slightly different meanings, some have different levels of formality).

1 Ask students to complete the exercise individually or in pairs. Allow monolingual dictionary use if necessary. When going over the answers, make sure that students can pronounce the words. Ask them to make a note of which of the words are more formal and which have slightly different meanings.

ANSWERS

1 i **2** h **3** a **4** f **5** g **6** d **7** e **8** b
9 c **10** j

Provide and *permit* are all slightly more formal than their synonyms; *adolescents* are people going through puberty so could be younger than 13, when teenage years traditionally start; *deal with* is just one sense of "manage"; you *nurture* a child, animal, or plant, but you can *foster* many other things, e.g., understanding, a feeling of happiness.

2 Students may need to use a monolingual dictionary or thesaurus for this exercise. They should pay attention to the meaning of words in order to choose the most accurate synonym for the context. They also need to be aware that some of the sentences might need to be grammatically modified in order to accommodate the synonym replacements. For example, in the third sentence, *lets us make* could be replaced with *allows us to make*, with the addition of *to*.

POSSIBLE ANSWERS

1 adolescents; worried; impact; society/planet
2 uncommon; virtual; ties/links
3 allows; form/create; relationships; diverse
4 unfounded; reduction/drop; face-to-face
5 character; appear; evolving
6 alone; get in touch with

3 For this exercise, students should first identify the repeated words, then replace them with synonyms. For students who are struggling, identify the words together as a class first.

POSSIBLE ANSWERS

The human brain is constantly changing, and neuroscientist Gary Small believes it is evolving further because of new technologies. He believes that our ability to multitask is improving. He says that our skills in making decisions are getting better. He also suggests that technology is developing our decision-making abilities. One study carried out with people aged between 55 and 76 using the Internet showed that the brains of the people who could already use the web displayed much greater activity than those of the people who could not already use it.

This is a good place to use the video resource *No man is an island*. It is located in the Video resources section of the digital component. Alternatively, remind students about the video so they can do this at home. Wiki groups can add some of these words to the class wiki.

Language development: Simple and progressive verb forms

Students will already know about the form of these verbs, but may still be making mistakes when choosing which form to use. Begin by finding out what students know about the two forms. Write *Simple and progressive verb forms* on the board. Ask half of the class to brainstorm examples of each and ask the other half to think about what the difference is in the use of each. Give them one minute, then ask for feedback. Refer them to the *Simple and progressive verb forms* box to find out if they were right.

Background information

Although verbs describing states are not usually used in the progressive form, there are many examples of stative verbs used progressively, especially in the media and in colloquial speech: *I'm loving it! He's feeling better. I'm not believing this! Are you doubting her abilities?* Students should be made aware that in formal English these forms are not used, but in colloquial contexts, they are acceptable.

1 Students should study the examples in the box and discuss why each verb form was used.

ANSWERS

The simple forms all describe completed actions. The progressive forms are all used to describe duration (*had been chatting, will be chatting*) or incompletion (*have been using*).

2 This exercise contains the verb forms in context—a useful way for students to see which form fits best. Ask students to first read the paragraph, then choose the correct verb form.

ANSWERS

1 have been carrying out (progressive emphasizes the incomplete ongoing action)
2 has shown (simple form to describe a factual action)
3 has helped (completed action; we see the result in the context)
4 has taken (completed action; we see the result in the context)
5 had benefited (completed action; we see the result in the context)
6 had used (completed action; we see the result in the context)
7 had then replied (completed action; we see the result in the context)
8 had been lacking (progressive emphasizes duration)
9 had begun (completed action; we see the result in the context)
10 will be adopting (progressive emphasizes the incomplete ongoing action)

3 Ask students to discuss their answers with a partner.

WRITING Writing an email

Background information

Writing an email at the appropriate level of formality to a college professor is a skill that many students lack. Students may omit the subject line or use an overly formal or informal tone. They may be unsure of how to address the professor or how to end the email. This uncertainty may prevent students from emailing their professor—a task which is acceptable and expected in most Western universities. In general, a formal or neutral tone is acceptable depending on the professor and the content of the email.

Begin with a discussion about the types of emails students send and to whom they send them. Ask students if they would ever consider emailing a teacher and if the tone should be formal, neutral, or informal. Find out what students think makes language formal or informal and write some ideas on the board to compare with the *Formality* box in the next section. Ask students to read the paragraph explaining what they are going to learn and what they are going to do.

Writing skill

Ask students to read the *Formality* box and compare the ideas on the board to the ones in the chart.

1 Ask students to follow the instructions. They should try to identify the features that make each text formal, neutral, or informal.

ANSWERS

1 Formal/Academic: writer to reader (formal language, e.g., *It is said that*; no contractions; *an increase in online communication*, i.e., noun phrase)
2 Formal: company to customer (formal, polite language; *product;* no contractions; no abbreviations, e.g.; *ASAP)*
3 Informal: colleagues (friendly, chatty style; contractions; slang, e.g., *gonna;* phrasal verbs; abbreviations)
4 Neutral: student to professor he or she is acquainted with (polite but friendly; contractions; phrasal verbs but no slang)

2 Ask students to rewrite the email extracts. They may wish to do this in pairs. Be prepared for students to feed back answers verbally, as there will be lots of possible answers, and evaluate the appropriateness of each pair's answers with the class.

POSSIBLE ANSWERS

1 Could you call me as soon as you can? I have a problem I can't deal with and need your help.
2 I'm very concerned that I won't be able to do my assignment in time and you won't be able to pass it. Is it possible for me to have an extension?
3 I'm Ahmed's friend. Ahmed suggested that you could help me with my research. Do you think that is possible?
4 I'm attaching a copy of my finished assignment, which I hope you enjoy. See you in class next week.

Cultural awareness

Formal emails in English generally begin with *Dear Mr/Mrs/Ms* (+ surname) and end with *Sincerely, Regards,* or *Kind regards.* (Remember also that American English requires a period/full stop after *Mr., Mrs., Ms.*) Informal emails can begin *Hi* (+ first name) or with no salutation at all. They may end with just the name of the sender or, if the people are close, with an X, signifying a kiss. Neutral emails may begin with *Dear* (+ first name) or *Hi* (+ first name) and may end with *Best wishes* or *All the best.* A too-familiar tone can cause offense, so it is best to err on the side of formality when unsure. Adopting the level of formality of the other person is another good strategy.

WRITING TASK

Background information

All the writing tasks in *Skillful* follow the pattern of brainstorming, planning, writing, sharing, rewriting, and editing. This process approach encourages students to think of writing as something more than just putting words on paper and will help them become more effective writers whose writing is more cohesive.

The brainstorming stage generates ideas, which is important in helping avoid writer's block.

Planning ensures that students have thought carefully about the content and structure of what they write.

Writing in class serves several purposes: firstly it ensures that students actually do the writing and that it is their own work. It shows students that the writing is an important part of the course. Secondly, it gives the teacher an indication of what students do when writing: do they look up words they will use first, or use a dictionary or translator while writing? Do they write, stop, count words, write some more, and keep adding sentences until they reach the right word count, or do they follow the plan they have made?

Sharing may take students some time to become accustomed to. Students are asked to read and evaluate each other's work. This not only improves students' editing skills, but also shows them that they can make valuable contributions—that it's not just the teacher who can judge a piece of work. In all units, students should refer to the Peer review checklist on page 109 of the Student's Book to help them review the work. Teachers can photocopy the page to give the students each unit. Teachers may also like to photocopy the *Unit assignment checklist* for each relevant unit at the back of this book for students to use once they are more comfortable with peer review.

In the rewrite and edit stage, students should consider their peer's comments carefully, decide on any changes they would like to make, and rewrite their piece of work. Many students will find this a new experience, but responding to feedback is an important skill to develop. You may choose to set this final stage for homework and ask that it be typed.

Ask students to read the *Writing task* instructions and discuss the kind of tone they think the email should adopt. Refer them to the box which outlines the audience, context, and purpose. Ask them how the email might change if the audience or context were to change. For example, if their professor is a man or a woman, someone from their own culture or from another culture, or if the context were to give information rather than request a meeting.

Ask students to read the email and do the task.

POSSIBLE ANSWER

Hi Joelle,
How are you? How was your weekend? Mine was hectic as usual!
Are you free later this week to get together and chat about the psychology project? I've been struggling with it and need a bit of help cos the deadline's fast approaching. I'm worried that if I don't get a move on, I'll end up rushing it. I really want to get a good grade for this one so need to put some work in.
How about tomorrow night? I've got an appointment in the afternoon but I'll be done by 6pm. Does 7pm sound okay? I can come to you if it's easier. I could even bring pizza if you like. Let me know asap.
Hopefully see you soon,
Allie

Brainstorm, plan, and write

Ask students how they would change the email to make it appropriate: use a more formal tone, avoid slang, avoid exclamation marks, etc. It is important that students realize that they mustn't simply change a few words. For example, how comfortable would they feel about asking their professor, *How are you? How was your weekend?* Or about telling her about the fact that his or her own weekend was *hectic*? They may choose to say, *I hope you had a good weekend*, or *I had a busy weekend* instead. It should also be pointed out that since they are asking the professor for a favor, they need to be a bit more formal. In addition, what do they think about suggesting a meeting at 7 p.m. or bringing a pizza? They may wish to suggest a time they are free or ask when the professor has office hours instead. They also may wish to apologize for the request—recognizing that the professor is busy.

Cultural awareness

University professors in the U.S. and U.K. generally have office hours when they meet with students either by appointment or on a drop-in basis. Students shouldn't expect to see professors outside these office hours unless a time has been arranged, and students should be sure to be punctual.

POSSIBLE ANSWERS

Tone—friendly but more polite and less chatty
Language—less slang and more neutral language, fewer phrasal verbs and abbreviations
Punctuation—no exclamation marks

Ask students to identify the key parts to the email that they need to include, for example: a greeting, an opening, the request, the reason for the request, a suggested time, an ending. Remind them of the audience and context. It may help some students to imagine an actual person—this will help them decide if they wish to write in a more neutral or more formal tone. Ask them to explain to their partner why they would choose a neutral or formal tone for the email.

Ideally, class time could be given for the *Write* task, with a set time limit—20 minutes, for example. The first draft can be written on paper, or, if the facilities are available, students can write an actual email which they would need to send to their partner for the *Share* section. They should aim to write 100 words.

Share, rewrite, and edit

Ask students to exchange emails with a partner. Encourage them to use the Peer review checklist on page 109 when they are evaluating their partner's email. They may write on each other's paper or make notations as appropriate. Encourage constructive feedback. If they don't think something works, they should say why. If they think something is good, they should say why. Give them about ten minutes to comment on each other's papers.

Ask students to rewrite and edit their emails. Encourage them to take into consideration their partner's feedback when rewriting. Rewriting can be done as an actual email: ask students to rewrite for homework and email you their finished request. You may need to specify a subject line, e.g., *Unit 1 request for a meeting*. Use the photocopiable *Unit assignment checklist* on page 86 to assess the students' emails.

Extra research task

Ask students to research email etiquette online. They should visit more than just one site to get various views and tips. Ask them to make a note of all the sites they gather information from and then come up with their own top ten email etiquette tips. They should bring their tips to class for sharing.

STUDY SKILLS Process writing and peer checking

Background information

Students not accustomed to process writing may be resistant to it at first. This section highlights why it is an important skill to develop. The *Scenario* section provides students with an example to critique while the *Consider it* section gives useful tips to think about.

Getting started

As a lead-in to the discussion questions, ask students to reflect on the writing that they did in the *Writing task* section: How did they feel about the stages they went through? Put them into pairs to discuss this question and the ones in the *Getting started* section. Once students have discussed in pairs, create a seminar-style discussion. If possible, arrange chairs in a circle so that students are encouraged to share and listen to each other's ideas. For question 3, challenge any students who think that the teacher is the only one who can give feedback to another student. Encourage them to recognize that their thoughts, ideas, and views hold value, and that they can give constructive and insightful feedback. This important skill is a step towards learner autonomy—a skill they will need as they progress, especially if they plan further academic education.

Scenario

Refer students to the picture at the bottom of the page and ask them to speculate on the writer's planning strategy: *Why has he put the information on so many cards? Why has he used color? What are the sticky notes for? Would this strategy work for you?*

Tell students they are going to read about Saif's experience. They should think about what he did right and what he could have done more effectively.

POSSIBLE ANSWER

Saif read the question carefully, he did lots of research, and he emailed his work to his teacher with a friendly, polite email. However, he spent only two hours writing the essay, he did not organize his work effectively, he did not ask a classmate to peer check it, and he gave his classmate only negative feedback.

Consider it

Students should first read the instructions and the tips, then discuss in pairs. Once students have finished, hold a seminar-type discussion to find out students' reaction to the tips and if they think they are relevant to writing in their mother tongue as well.

Over to you

This section could be done in pairs or as a whole-class discussion. At the end of the discussion, ask students if they have different ideas about what writing entails.

EXTENSION ACTIVITY

Ask students to prepare a graphic summary (a flow chart or other visual representation) of the stages of process writing and why they are important. You could ask them to research process writing further using the Internet. They should make their graphic summaries look nice so you can display them on the wall or bulletin board!

Reading	Identifying contrasts
Critical thinking	Identifying references to things outside the text
Language development	Guessing meaning from context Expressing contrast
Writing	Creating an outline

Lead into the topic by asking students to look at the picture and unit title, and speculate on how the two are connected. Find out if anyone saw the opening ceremony to the London Olympic Games® or any other big sporting event. Brainstorm other big events that are hosted internationally such as the FIFA World Cup (football/soccer), ICC World Cup (cricket), Davis Cup (tennis), Formula 1 (motor car racing), and non-sporting events such as the World exposition (World expo) and other international trade fairs.

Background information

The picture shows the opening ceremony of the London Olympic Games® in 2012. The ceremony, called Isles of Wonder, was opened by Queen Elizabeth II, directed by Danny Boyle, and featured music written by Underworld. The picture shows thousands of volunteers and spectators in the Olympic stadium, the Olympic flame, a copy of the London eye, fireworks, video screens, and spotlights.

Discussion point

Pre-teach *tournament* (synonym *competition*) and *drawbacks* (synonyms *downside, disadvantage, negative aspect*). Ask students to discuss the questions in pairs. Encourage them to give reasons for their comments. You could refer them to the functional language on page 108 of the Student's Book and ask them to pick out some functions or phrases they would like to improve during the discussion. As a follow-up, ask students to report some of their ideas in a seminar-type discussion. Invite students to ask each other follow-up questions and to comment on what other students have said.

Cultural awareness

Seminar discussions are common in Western universities, and the format is based on Socratic seminars. Participants are expected to interact with each other and the teacher by listening actively to each other, making relevant arguments, asking questions, and thinking critically. Levels of appropriate participation are often assessed as part of their grade for the course.

Vocabulary preview

In this section, new vocabulary is introduced within the context of a news article, with the definitions below. Remind students of the importance of trying to figure out words without looking them up and discourage dictionary or translator use for this exercise. (The *Language development* section on page 22 lists some tips for guessing meaning from context.) In order to raise student awareness about text type (text type dictates the tone and formality of a text), ask them what kind of text they think is shown and where it comes from (it's a news article from an online news source), and how formal they expect that text should be.

Ask students to complete the exercise, then compare answers with a partner. Ask students what clues they used to figure out the words. All the words have something to do with money, and more particularly about generating profit. For example, *revenue* could be guessed as something to do with money because the text talks about a big event in the town, tourists, and advertising. Big events draw tourists and advertisers who spend money.

ANSWERS

1 surplus
2 budget
3 financial
4 debt
5 gross domestic product (GDP)
6 return
7 exceeded
8 revenue

Unit 1 featured noun phrases as a feature of formal English. In this section, *gross domestic product* is an example of a noun phrase. Noun phrases are also very common in academic English, so it is worth pointing this out.

To reinforce the vocabulary, ask students to write sentences with each of the words, using the context of games. Allow monolingual dictionary use for this stage so that students can look up the word form(s) and any collocations. They could then read the full sentences out in pairs to check the context. If you are following the class wiki project (see the *Extension activity* on page 19), assign a group for this unit's wiki update. This would also be a good time to remind students of the extra vocabulary exercises in the digital component which could be assigned for homework.

READING After the Games end: Risks and rewards of hosting the Olympics®

Word count 1,150

Background information

The first Olympic Games were held every four years in ancient Greece starting around 776 BCE. They were not international in the modern sense, as competitors came from various Greek city-states. Originally, the only event was running. Winners received an olive branch and were treated with honor. Only males were initially allowed to participate.

The first modern Olympic Games were held in Athens in the summer of 1896. French educator Baron Pierre de Coubertin who founded the International Olympic committee is considered to be the "father" of the modern Olympics. He proposed the official Olympic motto: *Citius, Altius, Fortius* (*faster, higher, stronger*), and the Coubertin medal is awarded to athletes demonstrating a spirit of sportsmanship in the Games. In time, the Olympic Games grew to include the winter Olympics, first held in 1924 in Chamonix, France.

The Paralympics (*para* = *alongside*; Paralympics = alongside, parallel to the Olympics) also have an interesting history. People with disabilities were allowed to compete in the Olympic Games as early as 1904, but the Paralympic games as an official part of the Olympics grew with history.

Before you read

Ask students to think about the title of the report. Give them one minute to brainstorm some risks and rewards (not necessarily in association with the Olympics). Put them into pairs to compare their lists and to discuss their ideas before they read the questions. Then ask students to discuss the questions and feed back as a class.

Global reading

To lead into the identifying contrasts skill, ask students what the relationship is between the two lists they have compiled to elicit *contrast*. Ask students if they know of any other words that can be used to show contrast. Write these on the board. Ask students to read the *Identifying contrasts* box to find more.

SUPPORTING CRITICAL THINKING

In Unit 1, students learned about identifying the writer's argument. Writers also use contrast to build an argument. Often writers present the view that they disagree with first, then contrast it with a stronger view which is the one they support. Once students recognize this type of argument, they will be able to analyze it more carefully to decide the strength of the argument.

1 Ask students to read the instructions and check students understand what kind of writing a report is, who wrote the report, and who it has been written for. Ask students why they think the government committee has asked the consulting firm to write the report. Then give students five minutes to read the text and answer the question. Students should compare and discuss their answer.

ANSWER

b

a is not correct because Barcelona did build new sports venues, although they tried to build as few as possible.

c is a true statement, but it is not identified in the text as a significant difference.

d is also a true statement, but the text does not give it as much significance as the importance of planning for long-term costs.

2 Ask students to read exercise 2 and give them a couple of minutes to scan the text for the answers. Check answers with the whole class.

ANSWERS

1 Both cities	**4** Athens
2 Barcelona	**5** Athens
3 Athens	**6** Both cities

To reinforce the idea of contrasting words, ask students to go back through the text and highlight all the contrasting words they find. You could do this as a class by projecting the article onto the whiteboard using the Digibook.

Critical thinking skill

Exam tip

In exams, students often have to identify main ideas and supporting evidence in a text. Being able to recognize these and evaluate the strength of the evidence are also important critical thinking and academic skills. In writing for exams, students will need to demonstrate that they can support their ideas with evidence or reasons.

1 Ask students to read the instructions and check they understand what to do. Ideally, they will take notes on a separate piece of paper using a mind map or a hierarchical representation.

Students will need to read the text carefully to find the information, but should work quickly. Establishing a time limit will discourage students from becoming stuck on unknown words and push them towards faster reading skills. Remind students that they can look up words and read more slowly at home. Students can compare answers in pairs and discuss any differences.

Games

As an extension, you could ask students to read or paraphrase the evidence as you go through the answers.

ANSWERS

The three main arguments are 1, 3, and 4.
2 is not correct. The report argues that private businesses need to cooperate with public entities.
5 is not correct. The report argues the opposite, that increased prestige leads to more revenue from increased tourism and trade.

Evidence for the three main arguments:

1 Evidence of the value of having a clear goal includes Barcelona's clear goal of increasing prestige, which led to the important decision to minimize direct costs and focus on investments that would benefit the city for years to come.

3 Evidence to support the idea that it is crucial to prepare for the long-term financial impact include:
- It took Montreal 30 years to pay off its debt from the 1976 Games.
- Maintenance costs after the 2000 Sydney Games were $100 million per year.
- Barcelona spent relatively little (10% of its construction expenditure) on new sports venues so had minimal maintenance costs after the Games.
- Maintenance since the 2004 Athens Games has cost $775 million, and many venues have been abandoned.

4 Evidence to support the importance of a wide range of stakeholders include:
- Public and private entities cooperated well in the 1992 Barcelona Games, avoiding cost overruns.
- Stakeholders did not cooperate as well for the 2004 Athens Games, which led to delays and, in turn, caused the organizers to go over budget.

SUPPORTING CRITICAL THINKING

Students without much world experience can have problems understanding references to things outside the text. Building world knowledge will help students think more widely and make connections between events and ideas. Encourage students to read a broad range of texts on a range of topics to increase their world knowledge.

2 Find out where the students get information about what is going on in the world—through newspapers, online, via the radio, through social networks, through family discussions, etc. Ask them why they think it is important to stay informed. Refer them to the *Identifying references to things outside the text* box. See if they can think of an example of when they read something and understood the reference, and when they didn't. Point out that texts also might refer to information from history or science or literature, so reading across the disciplines is also useful. Ask students to complete exercise 2 in groups, discussing what they think the reference is to.

ANSWERS

1 Starting around 2008, many countries in the European Union had high levels of debt, including Greece.
2 "The chance to bring the Games back to their historic roots" refers to the fact that the Olympic Games originally began in ancient Greece.
3 "The events of September 2001" refers to the September 11th terrorist attacks in New York City and Washington, D.C.

3 This exercise can be done in pairs or groups so that students can discuss the reasons for their answers.

ANSWERS

1 No. The paper mentions "our better-known neighbours on the east coast." It is not clear which city this refers to, but we can infer that the city in the report is not as well known.
2 No. The paper says, "In this city, where a single sport captures most people's attention, there may be little long-term return on the investment in these venues." We do not know exactly what the "single sport" is, but we can infer it is not one for which a new venue is needed.
3 Yes. The paper refers to "the city's recent experience with the expansion of the art museum" as "an excellent base for cooperation."
4 It is most likely a rainy city or one with other sorts of weather that can delay events. The paper says, "Similarly, any city with weather like ours ought to plan for delays in events that are held outdoors."

EXTENSION ACTIVITY

To encourage students to keep informed about the world and about events outside their normal areas of interest, set students the task of accessing news on a daily or weekly basis. They should aim to access news from a variety of high quality sources and should try to inform themselves about topics they are unfamiliar with. Students should also read a variety of sources in order to compare types of reportage—this will help them develop their critical thinking. A few minutes at the beginning of each lesson could be spent with students in groups discussing what they have read.

This is a good place to use the video resource *Reality TV: the harsh reality*. It is located in the Video resources section of the digital component. Alternatively, remind the students about the video so they can do this at home.

Developing critical thinking

These discussion questions require students to review and retrieve information from the text before discussing their thoughts. For this reason, give students some time to take some notes and reflect on their answers. You could ask them to think about the questions for homework and come prepared to discuss them in the next lesson.

To help students prepare for the discussion and take good notes, draw a table on the board:

Potential benefits mentioned in the report	Potential risks mentioned in the report

Ask students to copy the table and fill in the information. Be sure to tell students to write the ideas from the text only, not to add their own ideas at this stage. Once they have identified a list, ask them to highlight or circle any they feel are significant and make a note as to why. Finally, ask them to add their own ideas, making sure to differentiate them in some way from the ideas they gleaned from the text.

For question 2, ask students to list the recommendations and highlight or circle the ones they think are most important. They should then give reasons for their view of the importance of some over others. Finally, ask them to add their own ideas as before.

In further preparation for the discussion, ask students to evaluate their success in discussions so far: Do they feel they participate enough? Do they feel that others listen to them? When they don't understand someone, do they ask for clarification? Do they try to help others speak by asking for their opinion? Do they listen and respond to others in the group? Do they give reasons for their opinions? Refer students to the functional language on page 108 of the Student's Book and ask them to identify another area they feel they need to work on during the next discussion.

Put students into groups for the discussion. As you monitor, try to pick out some good examples of successful communication, e.g., say *Jing, you gave a good reason for why the risk of … is significant. Juan, you really listened to Jing and asked good follow-up questions. Tian Tian, you opened up the discussion nicely when you asked who would like to begin.* This strategy will not only make them more aware of the kinds of things they should be doing in discussions, but will also highlight the importance of building good academic discussion skills.

If you are following the class wiki project, assign a group for this unit's wiki update. Ask them to include the academic keywords. You may also wish to give students a short vocabulary quiz during the next lesson. Read out some definitions or synonyms and ask students to write the word from the unit. Students can mark each other's answers or self-mark. Doing this on a regular basis may motivate some students to review vocabulary more often.

Language development: Guessing meaning from context

Exam tip

Students are not usually allowed to carry dictionaries into exams, so learning to guess unknown words from context and understand meaning without knowing every word will help students perform better.

Although students may have been working on building the skill of guessing meaning from context, this section highlights some strategies they can use to help them decipher new words. As a lead-in, ask students to tell their partner briefly what methods they use to guess a new word from the context. Ask them to read the *Guessing meaning from context* box to find some other strategies. Follow-up by asking students which point they think is the most helpful.

1 The sentences in the exercise are all from the reading text and practice the first two points in the *Guessing meaning from context* box. Ask students to complete the exercise, then look back at the text to check their answers. The paragraphs are listed for easy reference.

ANSWERS

1 overview **2** benefits **3** costs **4** prestige **5** exports **6** less popular

As a follow-up, ask students which are the synonyms (1 and 6) and which are the collocations (2–5). Ask students to discuss their understanding of the meanings of each of the words. It may help to write the collocations on the board: *benefits and risks; to incur additional costs; to confer prestige on; to boost exports.* Check they have understood the meanings.

2 This exercise practices guessing the meaning based on information given in the text. Students should match the words to the information, then check their answers in the text.

ANSWERS

1 b **2** d **3** a **4** c

3 Ask students to read each word in context and try to guess the meaning. They should discuss their ideas with a partner. Then feed back by asking students questions about the words to check they have understood the meanings: *Is $4.38 billion a large sum or small sum? So, what does "substantial" mean, then?*

4 Ask students to work out the meanings of the words in the box, then compare their answers with a partner.

Language development: Expressing contrast

Background information

In the *Global reading* section, students looked for ways the author expressed contrast. This section extends the skill of expressing contrast so that students can use it in their writing. Students should pay close attention to the structure of the example sentences, including use of commas. There are a few main errors that student make when using contrast words and phrases:

1. Sentence fragments: × *While costs are the primary concern for a host city.*
2. Run-on sentences: × *Cities must build expensive new venues however an Olympic host city must receive substantial revenue.*
3. Not recognizing *on the other hand, nevertheless,* and *nonetheless* as expressing contrast: × *Equestrian sports cost a lot of money; on the other hand, cycling equipment is expensive.*
4. *Despite* and *in spite of* introducing an independent clause: × *Despite hosting the Olympics is expensive, the benefits outweigh the cost.*

Remind students of the contrast language they looked at in the *Global reading* section and explain that they are going to extend this knowledge so that they can use it in their own writing. Students may be familiar with all the words and phrases for showing contrast, but still may be making errors in usage. Raise student awareness of the structures by posing questions to target their reading of the *Expressing contrast* box: *Which words introduce a dependent clause—a clause which cannot stand alone?* (*although,* (*even*) *though, while, whereas, despite, in spite of, unlike*); *Which words can come at the beginning or end of the sentence?* (*however, nevertheless, nonetheless*); *Which can be followed by a noun or noun phrase and a comma?* (*in contrast to, despite, in spite of, unlike*); *Which can have a semicolon before and a comma after to join two sentences?* (*in contrast, however, nevertheless, nonetheless, on the other hand*).

1 Ask students to complete exercise 1, referring back to the *Expressing contrast* box if needed. They can compare answers in pairs and say which rule from the box the sentence is following. Note that in sentence 2, *however* follows the pattern of point 4 in that it comes at the end of an independent clause. In this case, though, there is a second independent clause and the coordinating conjunction, *and.*

ANSWERS

1 In contrast to
2 however
3 However,
4 though
5 In contrast,
6 Despite
7 Unlike

2 Students can work in pairs or individually for this exercise, but they should write the sentences rather than just say them. To further emphasize the importance of correct punctuation, ask students to highlight the periods and commas, and say why they are used. Explain that poor punctuation can lead to lower marks in academic settings.

For further practice of the language development skills, ask the students to complete the digital component activities for homework.

WRITING A compare and contrast report

Background information

Compare and contrast essays are common in academic writing. There are a couple of structures that can be used in this type of essay: block or alternating. In a block essay, the arguments for one thing are put into one paragraph and the arguments for another into the second. This results in a four-paragraph essay. In an alternating essay, three main points are established, and comparisons and contrasts are made for each within each paragraph. This results in a five-paragraph essay. In this section, students will use a block structure. Note that compare and contrast essays need to have an argument. Within each paragraph, the idea that the writer is most in favor of comes at the end of the paragraph to make the argument stronger.

Writing skill

Find out if students have ever written a compare and contrast assignment, and if so, what they know about them. Ask them to read about what they are going to learn at the top of page 24. Find out how many students create outlines before writing and remind them of the importance of careful planning they learned from Unit 1. Ask them to read the *Creating an outline* box to learn about this skill.

SUPPORTING CRITICAL THINKING

Outlines help students think carefully about their main idea and supporting arguments. They can also help students clearly structure the details which support their arguments. Sometimes students can find it difficult to tease out which is the example and which is the argument. This can result in a paper which, to the reader, feels illogical. It is worth spending some time ensuring that the students can write an organized outline.

Cultural awareness

Essays in English follow a linear topical development, unlike in some other languages where topic development is circular or digressive. While studies indicate that some languages are adopting the linear development style, you may find that some students' writing seems "disorganized" due to a lack of a clear linear pattern. Helping students to create clear outlines will help them write in a more linear discourse.

Check that the students have understood the information in the *Creating an outline* box. Ask: *What's the purpose of an introduction? Why should each argument be a separate section in the outline? Why do you need details, examples, and reasons to support the argument? What does the conclusion do?*

Ask students to complete the essay outline.

ANSWERS
ii 1 c 2 e
iii 1 a 2 d, b
iv f

Once you have checked the answers, spend some time looking more closely at the outline. Ask: *Does the writer seem to feel that the World Cup is a positive or negative thing for countries to host? How do you know? Look at the introduction: What is the writer's thesis—the main thing he is arguing for? What are his two main arguments? How do the details support the main arguments? Does the conclusion restate the main idea and arguments?*

EXTENSION ACTIVITY

Ask students to create an outline for the article *After the Games end.* They will have to consider the main points and supporting details carefully, and this type of text deconstruction can help students internalize text structure.

WRITING TASK

Background information

A government white paper is a type of report which gives details about policies the government would like to implement. The white paper offers the chance for government to get feedback prior to implementation. Often white papers are turned into Bills put before Parliament.

Ask students to read the instructions and refer them to the box with the audience, context, and purpose. Take some time to discuss the writing task with the students to ensure that they know what they are supposed to do. For the task, they can choose which kind of event they would like their country to host. Ask questions to check understanding: *What kind of paper are you supposed to write?* (government report/white paper); *Who is your audience?* (people who will use the report to make decisions); *Why are you writing it?* (firstly to compare the effect that the event has had on previous countries; this information will be used to make a recommendation as to whether your country should host the event); *What is the topic?* (hosting the World Cup or other major event).

Exam tip

Students can lose points or even fail a writing task on an exam if they fail to understand and follow the instructions. Helping students deconstruct the rubric so that they fully understand what the task is asking them to do can help avoid this problem.

Ask students to look at the outline on page 24 again and answer the questions.

ANSWER
a is covered; b needs to be added to the outline

It is worth noting that only the positive aspects of hosting an event are detailed in the outline. Students may wish to do some research into any negative effects.

Brainstorm, plan, and write

Students need to take a step back from the outlines now and begin to think about the things that their country would need to do in order to host the event. They should consider their country's facilities such as stadiums, airports, hotels, trains, etc. For example, if there are no stadiums, then one may need to be built. The airport may need to be enlarged or accommodation (both for the athletes and the spectators) may need to be built. Transportation routes and means may need to be improved.

Using the information from the outline on page 24, the text on pages 20–21, and their own ideas, students should think about whether or not they would recommend hosting the event. Ask them to answer the questions in the *Plan* section, then discuss their answers in pairs before writing their outline. Remind students that there are two parts to the outline. In the first part, they need to compare the effects of hosting the event on two different countries—using the outline or the information in the text, or creating a new outline based on two different countries and/or a different event. In the second part, they need to bring together the points they covered in the *Brainstorm* section and the first part of the *Plan* section to create a recommendations section. They need to ensure that they link the points in part 1 to the recommendations in part 2—for example, *The long-term effects of the event on [country 1] were … and it would have the same effect on our country because*

… or *We saw that the benefits of hosting the event in [country 2] were … but in our country these benefits would be outweighed by potential problems such as …* Suggest they look back through the unit to find vocabulary words they may wish to use. When they have finished writing their outline, ask them to compare outlines and make suggestions for improvements. You could write some questions on the board to help this process: *Does the outline have an introduction? Does it have at least two arguments? Do the arguments have details, examples, or reasons? Are sources of this information listed where appropriate? Is the outline laid out in a linear, logical order? Does the outline have a recommendations section? Are the recommendations (part 2) linked to the compare and contrast section (part 1)?*

Give students some time to write the essay in class. Students should aim to write at least 300 words. The essay should contain headings as in the text on pages 20–21.

Share, rewrite, and edit

Ask students to exchange essays with a partner. Encourage them to use the Peer review checklist on page 109 when they are evaluating their partner's essay.

Ask students to rewrite and edit their essays. Encourage them to take into consideration their partner's feedback when rewriting. You could ask students to type and print out the final draft of their essay for homework. You might want to ask them to turn in their first draft, outline, and partner's comments along with their final draft. This will show you how much of the comments they took on board when redrafting. Use the photocopiable *Unit assignment checklist* on page 87 to assess the students' essays. This would also be a good place to ask students to complete the unit checklist in the digital component.

Extra research task

The article gives information about the effect of the Olympics on Barcelona and Athens. Ask students to research other cities which have held the Olympics to find out how the Games affected them. Alternatively, ask them to research other international events and their effect on the hosting city or country. Students should write up their findings in a short report, being sure to say where they got the information from.

STUDY SKILLS Finding an idea to write about

Getting started

Refer students to the picture of Hassan on page 26 and ask them what they think he is doing or thinking about. Introduce the topic of the section and put students into pairs to discuss the questions. When students have finished, ask several students to feedback what they discussed in pairs. Find out if the process is different depending on whether they are writing in their first language or English.

Scenario

Ask students to read and follow the instructions. Give them some time to think about their response, then put them into pairs to discuss. In the feedback session, write the ideas on the board that the students came up with. It may be worth pointing out that in most academic writing, students must acknowledge where they got their sources of information. Hassan was right to do a lot of reading, but should also keep track of the URLs of his sources to turn in with the essay.

POSSIBLE ANSWER

Hassan could have conducted more research and compiled notes before writing his essay. He also didn't stick to the essay title assigned by the teacher.

EXTENSION ACTIVITY

Refer students to the beginning of the report *After the Games end* on page 20. Ask them to highlight where the writer gives the sources of information. Why do they think the writer gives this information at the beginning of the report?

Consider it

Ask students to read the instructions and decide which tips Hassan kept in mind and which would have helped him. Ask students to add their own ideas to the list.

It's worth spending some time discussing each tip as a class, especially numbers 2 and 3. Tip number 2 is often difficult for students because, like Hassan, they don't have a clear idea of what they want to write about. In Hassan's case, he had a topic, but he didn't have a main idea or thesis. He hadn't formulated his argument. Discuss with students how the idea in tip 2 gives a clear focus to an essay because it provides something to build the argument on.

Tip number 3 shows students the difference between a topic and arguments. Point out that only the arguments state an opinion that can be defended with evidence, examples, or reasons. Tip number 4 is really about critical thinking. A good thinker gathers information and thinks about it, analyzes it, evaluates it, relates it to other things, and decides if it is actually valid or not.

Over to you

Ask students to work in pairs to discuss the questions. Ask students to try out some of the tips in their next writing assignment.

UNIT 3 NOSTALGIA

Reading	Understanding analogies in a text
Critical thinking	Identifying sources of information
Language development	Reporting information
	Condensing information with compound adjectives
Writing	Transition sentences

As a lead-in, divide students into four groups with different tasks associated with looking up the word *nostalgia* in their monolingual dictionaries. Group one should find definition(s); group two should write down the word forms; group three should look for synonyms; group four should go to the Macmillan Dictionary Online (www.macmillandictionary.com) to listen to and learn the American and British pronunciation of the word. Ask one member of groups one, two, and three to write their information on the board. One member of group four can teach the class the correct pronunciation of the word. Ask students whether they think the term has a positive or negative connotation in English. In general, nostalgia can be either, depending on the context; it has a bitter-sweet connotation.

Ask students how they think the unit title, *Nostalgia*, relates to the picture on page 27.

Background information

The image shows two young men, most likely brothers, holding up a picture of themselves as boys. The boys look happy, as do the young men. They may feel nostalgic for their younger days—maybe they had fewer cares, or maybe they remember the good times they had together as children. As adults, they may not be able to spend much time together, so they might be looking back with nostalgia at their younger selves.

Discussion point

Point out that nostalgia is related to memory. Brainstorm some differences between the two terms. Generally, nostalgia is connected to emotion as well as memory. Put students into pairs for the discussion. The first question relates to nostalgia, and the second two questions move into the area of memory. Be sure to encourage students to ask each other follow up questions to show their interest and extend the conversation: *Why was that time the happiest / the most difficult?* etc. Feed back some of the students' ideas on the board for question 3.

Vocabulary preview

Ask students to look at the pictures on page 28 and say how they are related to memory. The first picture shows a skull in which the brain shows up as blue, red, green, black, and purple. The brain is where memories are stored and retrieved. The second picture shows a baby in a pram and is related to remembering oneself as a baby.

Exam tip

Identifying the part of speech required for a gap-fill activity can help students complete this type of activity during an exam. It is common to find that students have written in a verb when they needed a noun, for example. This kind of mistake is easily avoided by taking a few minutes to consider the part of speech that goes into the blank.

1 To help with the exercise, ask students to identify the part of speech of each word, but without using a dictionary. Next, go through each word with the students to see if there are any clues in the words themselves that might give an indication of meaning. For example, the word *eyewitness* includes *eye* + *witness*. Next, ask students to identify what part of speech goes into each blank in the quiz, using grammatical clues.

Ask students to complete the quiz and compare answers with a partner.

ANSWERS

1 recall
2 eyewitnesses; stable
3 hippocampus
4 perceptions
5 short-term
6 long-term
7 neuroscientists

2 Students should now take the quiz, deciding which statements are true and which are false. The answers are given in *Global reading* exercise 5.

Students could also take turns to ask each other a question using each of the vocabulary words as reinforcement. Later in the unit, hold a "pop" quiz for students to self-evaluate their recollection of the terms.

If you are following the class wiki project, assign a group for this unit's wiki update. This would also be a good time to remind students of the extra vocabulary exercises in the digital component which could be assigned for homework.

EXTENSION ACTIVITY

You might want to do some work on words related to memory, especially the terms *remember* and *remind* which students often get confused about. Start by brainstorming words and word forms the students know related to memory, for example: *remember, memorize, recall, recollection, remind,* etc. Ask students to then look in their monolingual dictionaries to find more words to add to the brainstorm.

Students can then categorize their brainstorm by word form or they may wish to choose several examples to use in their own sentences. They can also look at the example sentences to see how *remember* and *remind* are used.

READING The shifting sands of memory

Word count 1,259

Background information

The expression *shifting sands* in the article title suggests frequent changes. Just as sand dunes shift and change with the wind, so memories shift and change. This is a metaphor because it likens memory to shifting sands. Writers also draw comparisons between things in a non-literal sense by using similes and analogies—both are types of metaphor, and both use the structure *X is like Y*. However, an analogy differs from a simile in that it is a logical argument—the writer points out how the two things are the same. So, the simile for the title would be: *memory is like shifting sands*, while the analogy would be: *memory is like shifting sands in that memories change frequently over time*. Analogies can help make more difficult subjects or concepts clearer. Whereas analogies are common in academic writing because they can make difficult subjects or concepts easier to understand, metaphors and similes are not encouraged in academic writing. This is because they can detract from the argument.

Ask students what they think the title *The shifting sands of memory* might mean and then to predict what the article might be about.

Before you read

Ask the students to discuss the questions in pairs.

Global reading

Cultural awareness

In English, there is an expression "to see the world through rose-tinted glasses" which means to see things in a positive light, optimistically, or better than they actually are. When the writer talks about *rosy memories*, he/she is alluding to this expression. In psychological terms, *the rosy retrospection effect* is remembering the past as better than it was.

1 Ask students to read the instructions, paying particular attention to the type of writing (article in a science magazine). Ask them what level of education they would expect readers of science magazines to have. Find out if they read any science magazines. Give them a few minutes to skim the article to find the sentence which best describes the writer's position. They should compare answers, giving reasons for their choice.

ANSWER
c

Refer back to the title of the article and introduce the idea of a metaphor. Show students how the metaphor can be stated as a simile by using *like*. Ask them to read the *Understanding analogies in a text* box to find out about another type of metaphor—the analogy. If any students are unclear about the difference between an analogy and a simile, explain that analogies explain the relationship between the two similar things. Analogies are common in all types of academic writing because they help readers understand difficult concepts.

SUPPORTING CRITICAL THINKING

Ask students to reflect on the content of the article and the target reader: why do they think the writer chose to use analogies in this particular article? (The article is from a popular science magazine read by the educated general reader rather than experts in the field. Analogies make the content easier to understand.)

2 Ask students to re-read the article and check the analogies that were mentioned.

ANSWERS
Analogies mentioned: 1, 3, 4

3 Students can work in pairs to explain the analogies.

POSSIBLE ANSWERS
1 Memory is like a video recorder because it captures everything we see and hear with perfect accuracy.
3 Memory is like a computer's hard drive because it stores and preserves memories complete and intact.
4 Memory is like a recipe because you recreate it each time you recall it, using different "ingredients" such as sights, smells, sounds. In addition, there are opportunities for error when following a recipe, and in the same way a memory can be distorted over time.

4 Students should look for the author's view here, rather than their own.

ANSWER
4; The author believes the recipe is the best analogy because it explains how a single memory is a collection of separate pieces or "ingredients" and why our memories can sometimes be inaccurate.

5 Ask the students to re-read the quiz from the *Vocabulary preview* section and decide which

sentences are true and which are false according to the article. This is an important critical thinking point—recognizing that different scholars may hold different views on what is true or not.

ANSWERS

Statements 2, 4, and 5 are true.

1 False. No one can recall being a baby because the part of the brain that forms these recollections takes a year to develop.
3 False. The hippocampus decides what to remember, but the memories are stored in many different parts of the brain.
6 False. Long-term memories often disappear or have serious inaccuracies.
7 False. However, they have done studies on drugs that help people forget things.

Critical thinking skill

Ask students why they think it is important to identify where someone gets information from. Find out where the students get sources of information and why they think these sources are credible or not. As an illustration, you could show students some websites to evaluate. Choose some .com websites to contrast to .org or .ac websites. Look at who wrote the information and what credentials they have. Next, ask students to find an Internet site they think is a reliable source of information and one they think is not. Ask them to say why one is more reliable than the other. The aim of this discussion is to get students thinking about validity of sources before asking them to read the *Identifying sources of information* box.

Cultural awareness

Questioning the reliability of sources is not something all students will be accustomed to. They may have come from a background where they were expected to accept information taught to them without question. In Western universities, it is common, and in some cases even expected, to question the professor. Challenging assumptions and received wisdom is one of the aims of Western education.

1 Ask students to read the article again quickly to find the source for each piece of information.

ANSWERS

1 the writer's mother
2 Elizabeth Loftus, a professor of psychology at the University of California
3 no source given; it's the author's own claim
4 Marc Green, an expert on memory and witness testimony
5 studies on memory show this; author does not say which studies
6 Karim Nader, a neuroscientist at McGill University
7 "other studies"—the author does not say which ones

2 Students work together to find three more pieces of information and their sources. When they have finished, ask them to compare with another pair to see if there are more examples.

POSSIBLE ANSWERS

"the results were dry and disappointing" (para. 2): the author's own opinion and experience
"25% of the subjects claimed that they clearly remembered the false incident" (para. 4): a well-known experiment by Elizabeth Loftus
"childhood memories have profound and long-lasting effects on our relationships with our family, friends, and spouses." (para. 5): no source given
"a tiny seahorse-shaped structure in the brain called the hippocampus plays a crucial role in deciding which events are worth saving as long-term memories." (para. 8): the author cites "researchers" but doesn't name specific ones
"a drug called propranolol reduced the intensity of traumatic memories of war and violence." (para. 10): a later experiment
"Loftus and her colleagues explain how they convinced subjects that they loved to eat asparagus as children." (para. 12): a study by Loftus called "Healthier Eating Could Be Just a False Memory Away"

3 This exercise can be done in pairs or small groups. Students should give reasons for their opinions.

ANSWERS

1 Answers will vary, but the most reliable information in exercise 1 is probably 2, 4, and 6 since their sources are experts in the study of memory and the brain. Information that is not sourced as completely (e.g., 5 and 7) may be less credible. Item 3 has no source but is probably true simply based on common sense.
2 You would usually not expect to find the writer's mother or the writer's own claims and memories used as sources in news articles or in academic essays on scientific subjects such as this one. In addition, in an academic essay, the writer would specify which studies (not simply "other studies") support her claims.

Developing critical thinking

Give students a few minutes to read the questions and reflect before getting into groups to discuss. If you find that some groups are not working very well, you could try mixing them up, or you could appoint a chairperson to lead the discussion. The chairperson would be in charge of inviting people to speak and making sure that everyone has a chance to voice his or her views. The chairperson should also control the discussion if too many people try to speak at once. After the discussion, you could ask students to evaluate their own role. Did they feel they were able to contribute, and why or why not? If not, what do they think they need to do to be a better participant?

As a follow-up, you could ask groups to give a short oral report on the advantages and disadvantages that they came up with.

This would also be a good time to remind students of the extra vocabulary exercises in the digital component which could be assigned for homework.

Also, this is a good place to use the video resource *Retro-volution*. It is located in the Video resources section of the digital component. Alternatively, remind the students about the video so they can do this at home. Students can also do the critical thinking digital component exercises for extra practice.

Language development: Reporting information

As a lead-in to this section, you could conduct an activity in which one student is the go-between for two fighting roommates and has to report what each has said. Divide the class into groups of three. Each group should have Student A, B, and C. Students A and B are the quarreling roommates and should sit opposite each other, but far enough apart so that Student C has room to move between them. The job of Student C is to listen to Student A, then report what he/she said to Student B and vice versa. This activity works best if the students agree on why they are arguing in the first place and see the activity as a sort of mediated negotiation since they are no longer on speaking terms. This activity can get rather noisy, but is an engaging way to introduce the idea of reporting information.

When the activity has gone on for a few minutes, stop it and allow students to move back to their desks for debriefing. Firstly, ask the mediators what words they used to say what the roommates had said. Write these on the board. Secondly, find out how easy the mediators found it to relay the information. Did they use the same exact words or did they paraphrase? What if one of the roommates said to say something rude—did the mediator try to soften the blow? How did the arguing roommates feel about the mediator's choice of words? Were they accurate? These questions highlight a couple of important points: firstly, that we use reporting verbs to give sources of information, and secondly, that we interpret and paraphrase what was said.

Ask students to read the *Reporting information* box and take notes on the key information it gives. Students should note that some reporting verbs are neutral while others express the writer's attitude. The second key point to note is the tense of reporting verbs. In general, writers use the present tense when reporting what the source of information says when the information is from a current book or article: *Nader argues that …* When reporting a study or a report, or something that happened in the past, the past tense is used: *(in his study) Nader demonstrated that … According to* generally shows that the writer has some doubt about the truth of something while *In fact* suggests agreement.

1 Ask students to complete the chart with the reporting verbs in the box.

ANSWERS
neutral: explain, say
has been proven: conclude, demonstrate, find, learn, show, state
has not been proven: argue, assume, believe, claim, indicate, suggest

2 All reporting verbs are not alike, and it is common for students to use the wrong reporting verb for the context. This exercise practices the skill of choosing the right verb. Students should compare with a partner, giving reasons for their choices.

ANSWERS
1 claims (because the report "offers no evidence")
2 found (because it is a "convincing" study)
3 argued; suggested (because the sentence implies that none of the studies have settled the issue)
4 concluded (because *believe* is used with people, not with studies)
5 show (because *learn* is used with people, not with data)
6 shows (because it goes with the adverb *clearly*)

3 This exercise reinforces the idea that *according to* is used when there is some doubt and *in fact* is used when the writer is more sure or agrees. It is also useful in helping students reformulate a sentence. Students should rewrite the sentences in exercise 2 using the reporting expressions.

POSSIBLE ANSWERS
1 According to the report, memory is reliable.
2 In fact, doing crossword puzzles improves people's memory.
3 The effect of caffeine on memory is still unclear; according to some studies, it has a positive effect, but according to others, this isn't true.
4 According to a recent experiment in Indonesia, elderly people who eat a great deal of tofu have a higher risk of memory loss.
5 In fact, a diet high in fish is good for people's memory.
6 In fact, people with long-term back or neck pain often have trouble remembering things.

Language development: Condensing information with compound adjectives

Background information

Note that compound adjectives are usually hyphenated when they come before a noun: *well-known actress; ice-cold beverage; fast-paced lesson*, but not when they do not modify a noun: *The actress was well known. My drink was ice cold.*

Lead into this section by writing the two examples from the *Condensing information with compound adjectives* box on the board: *… effects that last a long time; … a toy that you loved very much.*

Tell students that these phrases are too long, and you would like them to try to shorten them. Give them a minute to work in pairs to try to come up with a shorter version. See if anyone manages to shorten them using compound adjectives, then refer them to the *Condensing information with compound adjectives* box. Check students understand the difference between a compound adjective using a present participle and one using a past participle.

1 In this exercise, students have to show their understanding of when to use a compound adjective with a present or past participle. They can refer back to the explanations in the *Condensing information with compound adjectives* box for help. Note that in number 2, *heartbroken* and *heartbreaking* are one-word adjectives made up of a noun + participle, and so are not hyphenated. A quick check in the dictionary can help students find which words need hyphens and which do not.

ANSWERS

1 well-paid
2 heartbreaking; hard-working
3 pink-haired; brightly colored
4 smooth-talking
5 record-breaking
6 densely populated

2 This exercise presents a bit more challenge because students have to come up with the compound adjective. It might help students to identify the noun that is being described first and let them know the word order may change. For example, in the first sentence, *person* is the noun. Ask: *What kind of person? What kind of problems? What kind of name? Where should the compound adjective go?*

ANSWERS

1 Jane is a strong-willed person and rarely changes her mind.
2 Painful memories are often the cause of deep-rooted problems.
3 It's easy to remember Todd Splodd because of his odd-sounding name.
4 Because Jim is an open-minded person, he is always learning new things.
5 This is a never-ending documentary! When will it be over?
6 To remember the prefix *tri-*, think of a triangle or a tricycle, which is a three-wheeled bicycle.

WRITING Analyzing a memory

Ask students to read the information at the top of page 34 so that they know the purpose of the following sections. Ask: *Why do you think it is important to connect one paragraph to the next? What do you know about writing an essay?*

Background information

An essay differs from a report in several key ways. Firstly, essays are generally written for professors and should show a well-argued response to a question. Secondly, rather than giving recommendations, essays end with a conclusion which restates the main idea and arguments. Finally, an essay does not have headings—transitions and clear topic sentences distinguish one paragraph from the next.

Like reports, essays should have a main idea which is stated in the introduction. Arguments explaining, supporting, or developing the main idea should be backed up with details, examples, and reasons, so the outline structure learned in Unit 2 also applies to essays.

Writing skill

Ask students to read the first paragraph in the *Transition sentences* box to find out why a transition sentence is important and where it appears. Ask them to read the rest of the box to find out ways to write transition sentences. The example sentences in the box are from *The shifting sands of memory*. Ask students to find and underline the three example transition sentences in the text. For the first sentence, ask them to circle what *these findings* refers to in the previous paragraph. Ask students to look at the other paragraphs' first (transition) sentences in the article. How do they link ideas in the two paragraphs?

Exam tip

Examiners look for cohesion in essays, and one element of good cohesion is the student's ability to use transition sentences. Good transitions between paragraphs can increase a student's exam scores.

The exercise practices choosing good transition sentences. Although there are five options, only three are used. Ask students to compare answers in pairs, giving reasons for their choices, before checking answers as a class.

ANSWERS
1 b **2** d **3** c

EXTENSION ACTIVITY

Ask students to evaluate the source of the information in the essay. They can see that a woman named Elizabeth Loftus wrote a book describing an experiment. Do they know that the woman is qualified to write a book? What do they know about the experiment? How credible do they find the information? You could then assign them the task of finding out more about Elizabeth Loftus, her book, and the experiment she describes. They can then re-evaluate the information in the text. (Elizabeth Loftus is a distinguished professor of Psychology and Social behavior, Criminology, Law and Society, and Cognitive sciences who has written many scholarly articles and at least three books about memory. She is a credible source.)

WRITING TASK

Ask students to read the instructions and refer them to the box with the audience, context, and purpose. Take some time to discuss the writing task with the students to ensure that they understand the essay question. Point out that this is an essay supported by evidence, so they will need to report information from the texts accurately using their own words.

Cultural awareness

Using someone else's words without referring to the source is plagiarism. This is a very serious offense in Western universities. Students who plagiarize are sent before the Academic Conduct Officer, fail the assignment or course, and face the possibility of expulsion from the university. Ideally, students should paraphrase the ideas of others as well as referring to the source of information. If students use the exact words, they should use quotation marks and refer to the source.

Ask students to read the model text and follow the instructions.

ANSWERS

Although memories are generally reliable, research and personal experience both [suggest] that childhood memories are often less accurate. [According to] one [well-known] study by memory expert Elizabeth Loftus, up to 25% of subjects can have vivid, but false, memories of events that never happened to them. These findings are reflected in some of my own recollections. In one of my earliest memories, my mother fell asleep while we were coming home from school on a city bus. I remember being truly frightened. Would we miss our stop? Luckily, she woke up in time.

[According to] my mother, this memory is false. She [says] there were no bus routes near my school, and she found a [long-forgotten] bus map that [demonstrated] this fact. She also [claims] that she may have appeared to be asleep on another bus trip, but was only "resting her eyes."
These inaccuracies [show] how early memories can be distorted. Some details are likely to be true, while others are simply false, and perceptions from different times and events may have combined to form a single memory.

EXTENSION ACTIVITY

Ask students to create an outline of the model text, using the creating an outline skill learned in Unit 2.

Brainstorm

1 To begin, remind students of the essay question: *How accurate are memories?* You could put them into pairs to discuss this question briefly before doing the *Brainstorm* section. Next, students should re-read the texts and take notes on the evidence they find interesting while keeping the essay question in mind.

2 Ask students to follow the instructions, then share their lists with a partner. Encourage pairs to ask questions to stimulate more discussion.

Plan

It's a good idea to tell students to write the essay question at the top of their paper so that they can keep it in mind and not wander off topic as they plan. Review the *Writing skill* section from Unit 2. Ask students to create an outline for their essay using the points listed to help guide them, and referring to the model text if necessary. Allow plenty of class time for this important stage. Ask students to compare and comment on each other's outlines, then allow students to edit them as needed before writing.

Write

The model text is about 150 words long, but students should aim to write about 300 words. Draw students' attention to the key skills they should demonstrate in their writing: the use of good transition sentences, the use of reporting verbs to refer to the source of information, and the use of compound adjectives where appropriate. Give students time to write in class, but set a time limit.

Exam tip

Assigning timed writing tasks in class can help students practice writing under time constraints similar to exam situations. In exams, students will need to brainstorm, plan, write, and edit within a time limit. Although students learn to rewrite class assignments, they should be discouraged from writing first and second drafts in exams due to time constraints. Instead, they should plan carefully and create an outline to aid their structure. They should also leave a few minutes at the end so they can read over their work and make grammar corrections.

Share, rewrite, and edit

Ask students to exchange essays with a partner. Encourage them to use the Peer review checklist on page 109 when they are evaluating their partner's essay.

Ask students to rewrite and edit their essays. Encourage them to take into consideration their partner's feedback when rewriting. You could ask students to type and print out the final draft of their essay for homework. You might want to ask them to turn in their first draft, outline, and partner's comments along with their final draft. This will show you how many of the comments they took on board when redrafting. Use the photocopiable *Unit assignment checklist* on page 88 to assess the students' essays. This would also be a good place to ask students to complete the unit checklist in the digital component.

Extra research task

Students might like to do more research on memory which they then develop into a poster or PowerPoint presentation. Divide students into groups of 3–4. Give them some time to come up with a question about memory that they would like to research, for example, *How can we improve our memory? How do people study memory? What factors influence memory?* etc. Alternatively, they could research Elizabeth Loftus's work. If possible, arrange for students to go to the computer lab, or assign the task to be done outside of class time. They might start with a search for some of the studies listed in the articles from the unit.

CRITICAL THINKING SKILLS Eyewitness testimony

The purpose of this section is to get students thinking critically about the validity of eyewitness testimony. Begin by writing *eyewitness testimony* up on the board and asking students to briefly discuss any issues that come to mind regarding the topic. Ask them when they think eyewitness testimony is most often used. Brainstorm some situations on the board. How useful do they think this type of testimony is? How accurate?

Tell students they have been asked by the chief of police (you) to put together a report on the accuracy of eyewitness testimony. The courts rely on eyewitnesses, but the police chief is beginning to wonder whether the witnesses are reliable. Divide students into three groups. Group 1 is in charge of reading and summarizing the information from the *Untruth* section, group 2 reads the *Lack of expertise and insider knowledge* section, and group 3 has *The limits of memory* section. Give the groups time to read, understand, and discuss each section. Everyone in each group needs to become an expert so that he/she can confidently summarize the information from the section without looking at the text. Encourage students to take notes rather than rely on their memories!

Regroup the students so that each new group has someone from group 1, 2, and 3 in it. Ask students to share the information about their section, without referring to the Student's Book. In their group, they should prepare a short report for the chief of police explaining why eyewitness testimony is not very accurate and making a recommendation as to how to best use eyewitness testimony. For the recommendations, ask them to read and summarize the ideas in the *Corroborating sources* section. Appoint one speaker from each group to give you the report orally.

Extra research task

For homework following this section, ask students to research eyewitness testimony further (type it into the search engine). They may like to read about some of the studies that have been done, or they might look at some examples in the news in which eyewitnesses proved unreliable. In the class which follows, students can get into groups to report what they have found and read.

Reading	Summarizing
Critical thinking	Assessing whether research supports an argument
Language development	Adjective + preposition collocations Infinitive phrases
Writing	Avoiding plagiarism

Lead into the topic by asking students to look at the picture and unit title, and speculate on how the two are connected. Students will know the generic word *chicken*, but might not know that the male is called a *rooster* in American English and a *cockerel* (from which the term *cocky* comes) in British English. Females kept for laying eggs are called *hens.*

Cultural awareness

In the picture, the chickens are crossing a road, incurring some risk of being hit by a car. The scene alludes to a well-known joke in English: *Why did the chicken cross the road?* The answer to the joke is a statement of the obvious: *To get to the other side.* The joke is funny because it isn't—it breaks the expected pattern of having a punch line.

Discussion point

Put students into pairs to discuss the questions. As an alternative to question 1, students can create a risk questionnaire to ask in class. Ask pairs to write questions about the areas of life in the box, for example, *What risks have you taken at work?* or *Have you ever argued with your boss? Have you ever done an extreme sport such as paragliding?* etc. Students should then stand up and walk around the room asking different people their questions. This is a good activity for days when students are feeling lethargic or when you need a change from the norm. Be sure to have a feedback session where students can share some of the stories they have heard.

Vocabulary preview

As an optional lead-in to vocabulary work, students could review vocabulary from previous units. Hopefully, students will have been keeping a record of the vocabulary they have learned so far. Put them into pairs to quiz each other. This could help some students realize they need to review more.

Four of the terms in the box contain two words. Ask students to find them and feed back to you. Of the four, only *peer pressure* can be found in the dictionary—the rest are common collocations.

This illustrates again the importance of context to understanding.

Ask students to go through the words and identify the parts of speech, and then to identify the parts of speech needed for each blank in the text. This should help them find the right word for the blank. Tell them to try to complete the exercise before consulting their monolingual dictionaries.

ANSWERS

1 seek
2 disregard
3 consequences
4 personality trait
5 biological makeup
6 susceptibility
7 sound judgment
8 peer pressure

Make sure students are keeping good vocabulary notebooks by giving them a little class time to work on them. Check they have understood the words by doing a quick check. Ask: *Which word means …*

… the influence your friends have on you (peer pressure)?

… the results of our actions (consequences)?

If you are following the class wiki project, assign a group for this unit's wiki update. This would also be a good time to remind students of the extra vocabulary exercises in the digital component which could be assigned for homework.

READING Risk-takers: Who are they?

Word count 1,089

Cultural awareness

One of the dimensions of culture that culture-studies guru Geert Hofstede identified was risk avoidance. He found that some cultures tend to avoid risk and others tend to be more comfortable with it. Although Hofstede's models have their critics, evidence suggests that such tendencies exist within cultures, and a study at Ohio State University in conjunction with the Academy of Sciences in Poland showed that proverbs can shed light on how much cultures accept or avoid risk, and in which areas of life. In English, some proverbs encourage risk: *Nothing ventured, nothing gained. Who dares, wins. You can't make an omelette without breaking some eggs. You can't jump a 20-foot chasm in two ten-foot leaps. Fortune favors the brave.* Others encourage risk avoidance: *Look before you leap. Better safe than sorry. Once bitten twice shy. Better a thousand times careful than once dead.*

Before you read

Draw a mind map on the board and ask students to copy it. Give them a minute to think about a typical risk-taker and make notes, then ask them to compare with a partner. Get feedback from several students and fill in the mind map on the board as a class.

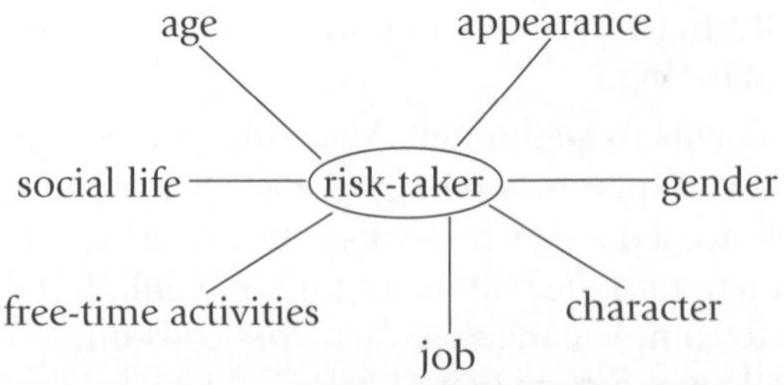

EXTENSION ACTIVITY

Put up some proverbs and quotes related to risk on the board for students to read and categorize—those which advocate taking risks and those which advocate avoiding risks. Ask students if they can think of any similar quotes or proverbs from their own language to add to the list. Alternatively, ask students to search online for quotations related to risk (type *risk quotations* or *proverbs about safety* into the search engine). Ask them to choose the quote or proverb they most identify with. Are they willing to take more risks in some areas (e.g., financial risks) than in others (e.g., social risks)?

Global reading

Summarizing is an important academic skill, but one that students find hard. Find out what students know about summarizing and what kinds of strategies they have before asking them to read the *Summarizing* box. Concept check to ensure students have understood. Ask: *Why should you skim-read first?; What kind of information should you note down?; What is the thesis in a summary?; Why should you include the name of the writer and date?* (because it needs to be clear where the information comes from, that it's not your own ideas);*Why should you use your own words?* (using your own words shows you have understood and also avoids plagiarism). Make sure students understand that a summary should never contain their own ideas, response to, or evaluation of the content. Find out how the guidelines for writing a summary in English compare to writing one in their own language.

If you find that some students have problems skim-reading quickly for gist, it would be a good idea to review some tactics such as reading the title and headings to predict content and structure, and focusing on nouns and verbs in the text rather than reading every word.

1 Ask students to read the instructions. They should note that the text is a research paper written by a professor, so it is going to be an academic text. Set the task, but establish a time limit—perhaps two minutes—to skim the text.

ANSWERS
2, 3, 4, 6

2 For the second reading, students should read the text more carefully, annotating and highlighting the text and taking notes. You could advise them to take notes in the outline format learned in Unit 2. They should then compare notes with a partner. Be sure to go over students' answers either orally or by writing them on the board. Ask students to keep these notes in a safe place to be used later in the *Writing task* section.

POSSIBLE ANSWERS
Biological reasons: dopamine—physical reason for risk-taking: neurotransmitter, linked to brain's reward system, people with fewer dopamine receptors = flooded cell = feeling of extreme happiness, research 34 men and women = questionnaire and brain scan found people with fewer dopamine receptors are risk-takers
Psychological reasons: sensation-seeking scale—psychological reason for risk-taking, Zuckerman's scale—40-item questionnaire to identify sensation-seeking people who are more likely to take risks, twin study showed 60% of sensation-seeking trait is genetic
Age: Giedd (NIMH, U.S.) study of brain scans 145 children every two years over ten years—results showed pre-frontal cortex (controls planning, judgment, reason) undeveloped until age 25—young people more likely to take risks
Gender: research Columbia Business School, U.S.—gender affects type of risk-taking—men take financial risks, and women take social risks, men and women seem to perceive risk differently

3 Ask students to choose the best thesis statement and defend their choice. Point out that the best choice is the one that is the broadest—the one that covers all the ideas in the paper.

ANSWER
The most appropriate is 2. 1 and 3 do not cover all the ideas in the paper.

Critical thinking skill

1 This exercise practices the skill of identifying sources of information learned in Unit 3.

ANSWERS
1 study at Vanderbilt University and Albert Einstein College of Medicine
2 Marvin Zuckerman's sensation-seeking scale
3 Zuckerman's twin study
4 National Institute of Mental Health, U.S., study
5 Columbia Business School research
6 Columbia Business School research

EXTENSION ACTIVITY

Ask students to identify the sources of information further by matching them to the bibliographic information in the list of sources at the end of the text. To do this they will have to analyze each source carefully. This activity will also help students assess the cited research in the next exercise while drawing their attention to the convention of bibliography writing. It will also help in the later writing exercise.
Answers: 1. Zald et al. (2008); 2. Zuckerman (1964); 3. Zuckerman (2007); 4. Giedd (2008); 5 & 6. Figner & Weber (2011).

SUPPORTING CRITICAL THINKING

Students need to be able to assess whether sources of information really support an argument and if they are actually the best sources to use. Sources are assessed based on currency, reliability, validity, and relevance. In choosing sources for research papers at university, students are expected to show they understand the importance of these four criteria.
Ask your students to look at the four areas and discuss in pairs why each one is important. *Currency* is important because new research leads to new discoveries. Older research is acceptable to cite, but be balanced with more recent studies. *Reliability* relates to whether the research can be believed both because of who conducted the study and because similar studies have yielded similar results. A study to determine how well a product works conducted by the company which markets the product would be less reliable than a study done by an independent third party, for example. This is important as it tells us whether we can trust the information. *Validity* relates to correct interpretation of results as well as how well the study was set up, and if it answered the questions it intended to answer. It tells us how useful and appropriate the results are. *Relevance* relates to choice of research, and how connected and important it is to the writer's subject. An article on financial risk management would not be relevant to the reading text, for example.

2 Students now assess the research identified in exercise 1. Give them time to think about the answers and then discuss them in pairs.

POSSIBLE ANSWERS

1 The sample is fairly substantial; it involved brain scanning, which can be considered objective; similar studies and results were seen in rats.
2 It was carried out by a respected psychologist; based on research with different types of people. Although not necessarily up-to-date, the scale is still used today.
3 The research was conducted with two types of identical twins and compared to research regarding other traits.
4 It was conducted by an official institution (U.S. National Institute of Mental Health).
5 The research has been done recently (2011) and therefore has currency. It supports the topic and gives reasons as to why people take risks. It is therefore relevant to the paper.

Developing critical thinking

Put students into groups for the discussion. Remind them of the functional language on page 108 of the Student's Book. If necessary, assign a chairperson for each group to facilitate the discussion. To follow up, hold a seminar-type discussion where groups can share what they discussed. For question 2, you might want to teach the term *nanny state*—this term has a negative connotation and refers to a government which is overprotective to the point of interfering with personal choice and freedom.

This is a good place to use the video resource *Risky business*. It is located in the Video resources section of the digital component. Alternatively, remind the students about the video so they can do this at home. Students can also do the critical thinking digital component exercises for extra practice.

Language development: Adjective + preposition collocations

Review the meaning of *collocation* (words that go together) with students. Then ask them to read the *Adjective + preposition collocations* box.

Background information

Students often ask why collocations exist. For example, we say *make a decision*, not *do a decision*, *willing to*, not *willing for* or *willing at*. The simple answer is because that's the way it's said. Students would also be able to find collocations in their own language. Adjective + preposition combinations are especially tricky because the preposition has no literal meaning. The collocation has to be memorized. Monolingual dictionaries can be used to find collocations, or students can note them down when they see them, and keep a list for reference and study.

1 Ask students to complete the sentences with the prepositions in the box.

ANSWERS

1 in	**7** to
2 on	**8** to
3 of	**9** of
4 with	**10** to
5 with	**11** for
6 in (note: in sth/with sb)	**12** in

2 Have students check their answers by looking back at the text. Ask them to highlight or underline the adjectives and prepositions in the text, then start a section in their vocabulary notebook to record them.

3 Ask students to work in pairs to discuss whether they agree or disagree with the statements in exercise 1. They should give reasons for their opinions. As a follow-up, you could do a class poll to find out how many students agree or disagree with each statement.

EXTENSION ACTIVITY

As a follow-up review, hold a class competition. Divide students into teams and ask them to decide on a team name which they write on the top of a piece of paper. Call out an adjective from exercise 1, and give teams 20 seconds to remember and write the preposition—without looking at notes or the book! Once you have read out all 12, ask students to swap papers to check each other's. Announce a winning team at the end.

Language development: Infinitive phrases

Background information

The infinitive + *to* construction often follows certain verbs and adjectives. Some common examples used in academic English are:

Verbs: *appear to; seem to; believe (something or someone) to; want to; tend to; refuse to; offer to; need to; intend to; fail to; cease to; decide to; plan to; agree to; advise (someone) to; persuade (someone) to*

Adjectives: *be likely to; be necessary to; be pleased to; be unable to; be prepared to; be (un)willing to; be difficult to; be (im)possible to*

Make sure students understand what an infinitive is, and elicit some examples of sentences containing infinitives with and without *to*. Tell students they are going to learn about three important forms of the infinitive which can change the meaning of a sentence. Ask them to read the *Infinitive phrases* box to find out what they are. Check they understand the meaning behind each example:

Perfect infinitive: What action took place before what other action? (the discovery took place before now); Continuous infinitive: What action is taking place these days? (taking more risks); Passive infinitive: What is more important: the linking or *it*? (the linking).

Draw students' attention to the forms of the verbs used with modals. Point out that modals often soften the strength of a statement in academic writing, so they are used to introduce academic caution. Compare: *It may be believed* … to *It is believed* …

1 This exercise asks students to identify the difference in meaning between the two sentences. Give students a few minutes to work out the differences on their own, then ask them to discuss them with a partner.

ANSWERS

1 Sentence 1 refers to the present (habit) and sentence 2 refers to the past.
2 Sentence 1 refers to the present (in progress) and sentence 2 refers to the past.
3 Sentence 1 refers to the present (habit) and sentence 2 refers to the past.
4 Sentence 1 is active and sentence 2 is passive; both use present perfect.

2 Ask students to read the text first to get the general meaning, then complete it as instructed. As a follow-up, ask them to underline the words that come before each blank.

ANSWERS

1 to be protecting	4 be needed
2 be given	5 to be missing out
3 to have learned	6 to have enjoyed

This would be a good time to remind students of the extra language development practice in the digital component which could be assigned for homework.

WRITING Summary writing

Ask students to read the information at the top of page 44 so that they know the purpose of the following sections.

Writing skill

Earlier in this unit, students assessed sources used for supporting an argument. This section looks at ways students can use sources in their own work, and highlights the importance of crediting sources of information.

Background information

Plagiarism is a serious offence in Western universities and can lead to a student being disqualified (not allowed to continue university). Students often wonder how teachers know they have plagiarized. Most professors will say that it is easy to pick out plagiarism. For one thing, professors know most of the sources that the students have read and will recognize the argument or views of the source. Secondly, the style of the plagiarized section will be different from the student's usual style. Many universities require students to upload written work into a plagiarism checker—technology that identifies the source of uncited phrases, sentences, or paragraphs.

Ask students to read the definition of plagiarism in the first section of the *Avoiding plagiarism* box. Spend some time discussing this important information, which may be quite surprising to some students. Next, ask students to read the five ways to avoid plagiarism listed in the box. Give them some time to read and digest the information before talking through each point.

The first point shows a way to reference using a reporting verb. You could take this opportunity to review the reporting verbs learned in Unit 2. Note that the reporting verb is in the present tense.

For the second point, make sure students understand *quotation* and *quotation marks*. You might want to point out that quotations should be used sparingly.

For the third point, look at the three different examples. The first sentence is the original text. The third sentence is a good example of paraphrase for two reasons. First, the student has used his own words, but perhaps more importantly, has shown that he understands the original because he can put it into his own words.

The fourth point shows how to reference a source that is referenced in another work. This is an important point that students may be surprised by. Ideally, a student will find the original source, but this is not always possible. You may need to teach the term *to cite*: when you use someone else's ideas or words and reference the source, you are *citing* the source. In the example, Roberts is the book that the student read, and in it, Roberts cited Stirling.

The fifth point refers to a bibliography. A bibliography is a list of all sources cited in a text. There are many different systems for writing bibliographies, and students should follow the style required on their courses when they are in Higher Education. Systems include the Harvard system APA, and MLA.

In APA and MLA, the main difference between the systems is the order in which information is displayed and punctuated, but the content is the same: they all have the name of the author, date of publication, name of the book or article, name of the journal the article is found in, the issue and volume number (journals), and the publisher (books).

EXTENSION ACTIVITY

Ask students to look back at the text on pages 40–41 and highlight or note down the different ways that the author has cited sources. They may note that in the fifth paragraph, no reporting verb is used. This is another way to cite a source—by putting the author's last name and the date the work was published in parentheses at the end of the sentence.

Cultural awareness

Students cannot always differentiate between first name and last name, and so may write in their bibliography: *Stacey, H.* instead of *Hughes, S.* Ensure students understand that *last name* refers to the author's family or surname. One way to tell which is which is to look for a comma. If the name is listed with a comma: *Hughes, Stacey*, then the last name is first. If there is no comma: *Stacey Hughes*, then the surname is second.

1 The exercises take students through the steps of summarizing a short text. For exercise 1, students should read the excerpt and briefly state the topic.

ANSWER
The topic is peer pressure and its effect on teenage drivers.

2 Ask students to read and follow the instructions. They should use their own words in the thesis statement.

ANSWER
Main argument: Peer pressure affects teenage drivers, which may explain the higher number of accidents among teenagers.
Supporting argument: In a study, teenagers showed that they were willing to take more risks when they thought friends were watching.
Student's own ideas for the thesis statement.

3 This exercise helps students see how plagiarism can occur. Ask students to discuss their views in pairs.

ANSWER
The writer is not sourced; there is no date of the author's work; much of the text is copied and not paraphrased; the study is not named, dated, or sourced.

4 In this exercise, students use their notes to summarize the excerpt. This is good practice because it helps students avoid copying. Note that the summary should be much shorter than the original, so ensure students only write two or three lines. The source information is found in the instructions for exercise 1.

POSSIBLE ANSWER
Dr. Bauman (2013) suggests that teenage drivers may be influenced by pressure from friends. A Temple University study found that teenagers playing a computer driving game were more likely to take risks when they thought that same-sex friends were watching them, explaining why more accidents are caused by teenagers than other age groups.

Extra research task

Ask students to research plagiarism on the web. They could find out more about what plagiarism is (search *what is plagiarism*), or more ways to avoid it (search *avoiding plagiarism*), or even more about intellectual property. If they are planning to go to a specific university, they could find out what that university's plagiarism policy is.

WRITING TASK

Ask students to read the instructions and refer them to the box with the audience, context, and purpose. Point out that summary writing is quite a common way professors assess whether students have understood information they have read or heard in lectures.

Ask students to read the example summary and follow the instructions.

ANSWERS

In her article "The need to learn risk" (2013), which can be found in the *Journal of Risk Literacy* (Vol. 2, Issue 4), Patricia Hughes argues that risk literacy is essential in our daily lives and therefore should be studied in schools in order to help young people to calculate risk better, suggesting ways in which risk literacy could be taught. To support her argument, Hughes provides evidence that risk literacy education has been successful among 16-year-olds. One hundred 16-year-olds were involved in her study, which required them to make decisions about how to save or invest money both prior and subsequent to receiving lessons on statistics. The teenagers appear to have been more successful in making decisions based on calculated risk after their lessons, which prompted Hughes to say that "secondary schools should be doing more to teach risk literacy in math lessons."

Yes, it has been sourced appropriately.

Brainstorm, plan, and write

Students should try to remember the steps for writing a summary, but may look back at the steps on page 38 if they need to jog their memory.

ANSWERS

Step 1: Skim-read the text.
Step 2: Reread the text carefully and take notes.
Step 3: Write a thesis statement.
Step 4: Write the summary using your own words. Include a thesis statement plus your own ideas.

Ask students to look back at the thesis statement they chose in exercise 3 on page 38 and find the notes that they took in exercise 2. They will use these to write their summary. You may want to allow them to use the thesis as is rather than changing it into their own words. In this planning stage, students should choose the information to include and organize it into an outline. They can use the model summary to help in the organization, but will need to write about 300 words, which is twice the length of the model. Students may wish to plan where they will use adjective + preposition collocations and infinitive forms. Ask students to compare outlines for their summaries before writing.

Give students about 30 minutes to write their summary. Teach them how to assess word counts quickly: count the number of words on a line and multiply by the number of lines.

POSSIBLE ANSWER

Wittman (2012) believes that age, gender, character, brain, and genetic makeup can all help to determine whether a person is a risk-taker.

A joint study at Vanderbilt University and Albert Einstein College of Medicine demonstrated that the chemical associated with pleasure in our brains can impact on risk-taking activities. People whose brain cells had fewer active dopamine receptors were bigger risk-takers. As the receptors are unable to prevent a cell from becoming flooded with dopamine, a strong feeling of excitement is felt. It is therefore likely that people with fewer receptors try to repeat this feeling by taking more risks.

The pre-frontal cortex part of the brain may also impact on risk-taking activities. This is the part of our brain that deals with reason. Research carried out at the National Institute of Mental Health showed that it may not fully form until a person is 25. This may affect a person's judgment and cause him or her to take more risks.

Our personalities may also be a factor in risk-taking. In the 1960s, Marvin Zuckerman identified the sensation-seeking personality trait. In research with identical twins, he found that 60% of this trait is inherited. As with dopamine, people who are sensation-seekers may take more risks as they attempt to find new and exciting activities.

Finally, the types of risk that a person takes may be affected by gender. Research by Columbia Business School suggests that men are more likely to take financial risks, whereas women tend to take social risks. The researchers also claim that risk is perceived differently depending on a person's life experience and that this may be affected by gender.

Although Wittman does not identify one specific cause of risk-taking, all of the research above indicates that there could be a number of causes.

Share, rewrite, and edit

Ask students to exchange their summaries with a partner. Encourage them to use the Peer review checklist on page 109 when they are evaluating their partner's summary. If students want to see an example summary, you could photocopy the one above for the students to see. Students should understand, however, that it is not the "right" answer, as there are many ways to write the summary. You may wish not to show them the summary, but use it as reference when marking the students' papers. If you do show the students, be sure to take the copies off them before asking them to rewrite and edit their own summaries, so that they do not copy the example summary!

Ask students to rewrite and edit their summaries. Encourage them to take into consideration their partner's feedback when rewriting. You could ask students to type and print out the final draft of their summary for homework. Use the photocopiable *Unit assignment checklist* on page 89 to assess the students' summaries. This would also be a good place to ask students to complete the unit checklist in the digital component.

Extra research task

Ask students to find examples of posters, infomercials, etc. which are designed to teach people to make safer decisions in life. Examples might include anti-smoking campaigns or ads encouraging people to buckle up. Students should decide what the risk is, who is funding the campaign, and who it is aimed at. They can bring in photos of posters or downloads of infomercials to show each other in groups. As a class, assess whether or not these campaigns are likely to be successful.

STUDY SKILLS Evaluating online sources

Background information

With so much information on the web, it is easy to accept information as true without considering the source. Web users need to understand that anyone can post anything on the web and then that information can be reposted to create modern-day urban myths. This section aims to raise student awareness about reliable sources. In general, *.com* sources are less reliable than *.org*, *.ac*, *.net*, and *.gov* sites, and using a search engine which focuses on academic work will yield more appropriate results.

Getting started

Put students into pairs to discuss the questions. Ask several students to feed back to the rest of the class.

Scenario

Ask students to read the scenario and decide what Liliana did right and wrong. They should give reasons for their opinions.

POSSIBLE ANSWER

Liliana accessed academic websites; she made notes as she did her research and recorded the web addresses so she could find/source them later; and she sourced the work in her essay. However, she looked only at the first ten websites she found; she looked only for information that supported her point of view; and when she wrote her essay, she presented just one argument. Finally, not all her supporting information was valid and reliable. She did not know where all the information came from, and the information presented by the road safety campaign website may be biased.

Consider it

Ask students to read and discuss the tips. As a follow up, explore the tips further with added discussion questions, e.g., ask: *Why should you provide different views? How do you know if a site is academic? Where can you find out about the author? How can you make sure you stay on topic during searches? What are some easy ways to keep a record of websites?*

Over to you

Ask students to discuss the questions, then hold a seminar discussion with the class to share answers. Write down some of the students' tips and ideas for useful web programs or apps. You could ask students to do some research to find and assess other useful programs or apps.

Background information

There are some online applications which can help you record the information you are reading for your academic study. Useful apps include Endnote, Scrible, and Evernote.

Extra research task

Ask students to find out how to write a bibliographic entry for a website.

UNIT 5 SPRAWL

Reading	Identifying different perspectives
Critical thinking	Recognizing trends and patterns
Language development	Prepositional phrases
	Impersonal report structures
Writing	Hedging

Lead into the topic by asking students to look at the picture and say what they see. You may need to introduce the terms *spire* and *skyscraper*. Ask students why they think urban planners build skyscrapers and if they improve or detract from urban life. Encourage students to give reasons for their views. Ask students to look up the word *sprawl* in their monolingual dictionaries to find the definition that best fits the context of the picture (growth or expansion of urban areas). Does it have a negative or positive connotation in this context? (It is usually negative as it connotes unchecked or poorly planned growth.)

Background information

The picture depicts the tops of some of the many skyscrapers in Dubai. The Burj Khalifa, at its completion in 2010, was the tallest building in the world, standing at 2,717 feet (828 meters). Inside there are offices, retail stores, hotel facilities, and residential dwellings on its 163 floors. The Princes Tower, currently the world's tallest residential building, is 1,358 feet tall (414 meters) and has 101 floors, including six floors of underground parking and several retail outlets.

Discussion point

Put students into pairs to discuss the questions. In the feedback session, you could ask students to compare and contrast the dwellings suggested in the picture on page 47 to the dwellings shown on page 48. This will recycle some of the language for contrasting expressions learned in Unit 2.

Vocabulary preview

1 Ask students to try to match the definition halves by using context and grammatical clues. After comparing answers, ask students to think of examples for each word or phrase: *The government rehoused villagers when they built the dam; Greenpeace is an environmental NGO and Habitat for Humanity is a charitable NGO*; etc. You also might ask students to identify the part of speech of each term and make a word form chart for the other forms of each word in order to build their flexibility with the terms.

ANSWERS
1 c **2** g **3** d **4** a **5** f **6** e **7** h **8** b

2 Discuss the questions in a class seminar format. Encourage students to give reasons for their answers, listen, and respond to each other.

If you are following the class wiki project, assign a group for this unit's wiki update. Remind them to be sure to include the academic keywords from the text, too. This would also be a good time to remind students of the extra vocabulary exercises in the digital component which could be assigned for homework.

READING Solving the problem of informal settlements

Word count 1,016

Background information

It is easy to think of informal settlements as vast sprawling areas of poverty. However, NGOs such as the Cambodia-based Sahmkaum Teang Tnaut (STT) are helping communities grow stronger through participatory mapping and enumeration activities. These raise the profile of the communities, making them visible to government which otherwise wouldn't count them in the census. As importantly, they serve to raise policy legislation awareness, confidence, and solidarity within the community. When relocation of these communities is inevitable, mapping and enumeration helps these poor communities prepare for their relocation, giving them a more informed platform from which to negotiate.

Before you read

Refer students to the picture on page 48. Ask them to work in pairs or small groups to discuss the questions. To find other English terms for *informal settlements*, ask students to scan the first paragraph of the text on page 50. See who can find the three terms the fastest (*slums, shanty town, favelas*).

Exam tip

Students can predict content by understanding how articles are structured. The first paragraph generally gives an overview of the article, and the thesis or main point can often be found at the end of the introduction. Headings summarize the sections they precede. The final paragraph concludes the main ideas. By reading the title, first and last paragraphs, and conclusion, students can get a very quick overview of the article which will enable them to work through exam questions more quickly.

Similarly, by understanding the type of essay: comparison/contrast, problem/solution, cause/effect, historical, classification/division, descriptive, etc., students can predict which parts of the text will give which information. This makes reading faster and finding answers to comprehension questions more efficient.

Ask students to read the title and predict what type of text this is: comparison/contrast, problem/solution, cause/effect, or classification/division. Since the title contains the words *solving the problem of*, students can guess that it will be a problem/solution essay. Ask them which section is likely to contain the solution (the conclusion), which are likely to contain the problems (the middle sections), and which is likely to contain the background (the introduction).

Ask students to read the last sentence in the introduction and say what the solution is that the writer will discuss (rehousing), and what three areas he will touch on (wealth, health, and the environment). Point out that these three areas are also the headings used in the article. Ask students to read the conclusion. Is the writer in favor of or against rehousing? (The writer is in favor.)

The sources listed at the end of the article are all from internet sources. To review and extend the study skills learned in Unit 4, refer students to the source list. Ask them to assess the sources. Ask: *How many different sources were used? What makes them appropriate sources?* (Most are from reputable *.org* sites or from reputable news sources; they are relevant to the topic.) Ask students to note the information required in a bibliography for an online source: name, date, title, when retrieved, URL.

Global reading

Lead into the idea of different perspectives by asking several students: *What is your viewpoint or perspective on people who cannot afford proper housing?* Point out that each student has a different perspective. Ask students to read the *Identifying different perspectives* box to find out why this is important in academic settings. Check to make sure students have understood why it is important to identify different perspectives in a text and why it is important for the writer to include them.

SUPPORTING CRITICAL THINKING

Understanding multiplicity of perspective is important to cognitive development and a higher-order critical thinking skill. In addition, this understanding of different perspectives can lead to people becoming more global citizens.

1 Ask students to read the instructions and take note of the writer, purpose, and context stated. Give students a few minutes to read the text more closely and answer the question.

ANSWER

Rehousing people means taking them away from their existing community and giving them housing in a different area. Upgrading settlements involves trying to improve people's existing housing and community.

2 There are several groups of people listed in the text. Ask students to underline them.

ANSWERS

residents, government, middle-class families, youth, nearby city residents, NGOs, Mumbai citizens

3 Students might like to copy the table into their notebooks so that they have more room to write. Ask students to compare answers in pairs. Ask early finishers to put the answers in a table on the board.

ANSWERS

	Rehousing	Settlement upgrading
Informal community residents	better economic situation / access to services such as water, etc.	keep in touch with the community / more work opportunities / cheaper rent
Governments	reclaim land / bring residents into the mainstream—pay taxes	more economically viable / less money is spent on infrastructure
Other city residents	own house value no longer affected	would retain the benefits of having nearby existing dwellers offering services such as recycling
NGOs	affects psychological health of residents	build on community spirit and informal economies

4 The answers to this exercise are not all overt, so students may need to infer to work out the answers.

ANSWERS

1 B **2** U **3** B **4** R **5** R **6** B

Critical thinking skill

To lead into this section, ask students about the trend of urbanization: is it increasing or decreasing? Refer them to the *Recognizing trends and patterns* box to find out how to identify each. Check to make sure they understand the difference between the two terms. Ask: *Which describes habitual events?* (patterns); *Do trends describe increases or decreases?* (both). Make sure students understand the term *vague*. Ask: *Is vague language precise/exact or approximate?* (approximate).

SUPPORTING CRITICAL THINKING

You may need to point out the difference between *by X%* and *to X%*. *By* indicates the amount of change while *to* indicates the final amount.

1 Ask students to complete the sentences with figures from the text.

ANSWERS

1 five billion, 3.3 billion	5 80
2 Nearly one billion	6 Around 85
3 500 million	7 700 million
4 60	8 two billion

2 Students should decide which of the figures they inserted into the previous exercise represent trends, patterns, or static figures.

Exam tip

Learning to scan quickly for information can help students on exams where time is limited. To help with scanning skills, tell students not to scan left to right because the mind tends to try to read and make meaning rather than target words (or in this case, numbers). Tell them to try scanning from right to left or starting at the lower left-hand corner of the text and moving upwards in a diagonal to the top, then down in a diagonal to the lower right-hand corner. This tricks the mind into not reading, but into looking for single units of meaning.

ANSWER

1, 3, and 8 are trends; 4 is a pattern. The others are static figures.

Developing critical thinking

Give students a few minutes to read the questions and reflect before getting into groups to discuss. Appoint a chairperson as needed and refer students to the functional language on page 108 of the Student's Book. As a follow-up, you could ask groups to give a short oral report on their ideas for what governments can do to prepare for urbanization.

This is a good place to use the video resource *The urban footprint*. It is located in the Video resources section of the digital component. Alternatively, remind the students about the video so they can do this at home. Students can also do the critical thinking digital component exercises for extra practice.

Language development: Prepositional phrases

Begin by reviewing the grammatical terms: *preposition, noun, pronoun, adjective, adverb, gerund, noun clause, noun phrase.* Make sure that students understand the difference between a noun phrase and a noun clause. A noun phrase is a group of words that go with the noun: *the biggest advantage* is a noun phrase consisting of an article, *the*; an adjective, *biggest*; and a noun, *advantage*. A noun clause is a dependent clause (with a subject and verb) that functions as a noun: *that I saw yesterday*. Noun clauses can start with *that, who, which, what, where, when,* and *how*. Brainstorm examples of each on the board, then ask students to read the *Prepositional phrases* box.

Ask students in pairs to write another example of each structure.

Check to make sure students understand that the phrase *with no secure tenancy rights* functions as an adjective because it modifies *land*: *What kind of land? Land with no secure tenancy rights.* You might need to draw a parallel with a more familiar adjective. Use the same sentence, but substitute *unsuitable land*. Ask the same question: *What kind of land? Unsuitable land*, to show how the adjective functions the same.

Next, check students understand how the prepositional phrase functions as an adverb in the example: *Their aim is to drive economic development why? With a view to …*

1 Ask students to find the prepositional phrases in the text and underline or highlight them. Note that some prepositional phrases end in a preposition, e.g., *in the event of*.

2 Ask students to use the prepositional phrases in the box in exercise 1 to complete the text.

ANSWERS

1 On the face of it (used to introduce something that appears to be true but may not be when closely examined)
2 by no means (emphasizes a negative statement)
3 in response to (in answer to)
4 In terms of (in relation to / with reference to)
5 in favor of (support an idea)
6 In the event of (used to say what will happen in a future situation)
7 on the increase (increasing)
8 In light of (because of)

EXTENSION ACTIVITY

Ask students to take notes about the positive aspects of city dwelling listed in the excerpt. Set the challenge of summarizing the text in two or three sentences to practice summarizing skills learned in Unit 4. As another alternative, you could stage a mini debate about city dwelling using the ideas from the excerpt and the article on pages 50–51.

3 This exercise looks at understanding the meaning of common prepositional phrases. Students should match the phrases with the definitions.

ANSWERS
1 d 2 c 3 a 4 e 5 b

4 Students can do this exercise orally or in writing. If students are struggling to think of ideas, ask them to first write the sentences, then read them to a partner. Ideally, use this exercise as an opportunity for students to think quickly and speak.

Language development: Impersonal report structures

To lead into this language area, ask students what they can say in an essay when the information they are reporting is widely believed. Give a topic example such as immigration or urbanization to help spark ideas. Students may come up with something along the lines of *People think that urbanization* … or *Many people believe that immigration* … Tell them they are going to learn a more academic, impersonal way to describe widely accepted information. Make sure they understand that *impersonal* is the opposite of *personal*—in some types of academic writing, it is more common to be impersonal—not using *I* or *we*, for example. Refer them to the *Impersonal report structures* box. Ask them to highlight the three structures.

1 Ask students to rewrite the sentences, starting with the words in parentheses. You may need to model the first sentence on the board. It may also help students to identify the verb that they will be using first (*know, suppose, think*, etc.).

ANSWER
1 It is known that people are unable to find work in rural areas.
2 Living in a city is supposed to bring more employment opportunities (for people).
3 There is thought to be greater access to schooling.
4 It is believed that transport is much better in the city.
5 There are estimated to be 70 million people moving to cities each year.
6 Urban life is alleged to be worse for migrants (by some people).
7 It is claimed that this is not true and rural life is far worse.
8 Urbanization is said to be necessary for a country to develop.

Cultural awareness

Impersonal reporting structures are used more in written English than in spoken English, except in very formal situations. Written English that tries to be more chatty—many magazine articles or even online news articles, for example—would use a more personal style to make the reader feel like the writer is talking to him or her.

2 Ask students to complete the sentences in writing. If you want to add an element of interest, tell students to write four true sentences and one false sentence.

3 Ask students to share their sentences with a partner. Tell them to be convincing in their explanations so that their partner can't guess which is the false sentence, if you have followed this procedure. The "winner" of the pair is the one who can spot the false sentence. Pairs can decide together whether or not the reputation of the described cities is fair or not. Many widely held beliefs are based on stereotypes and are not really fair assessments.

This would be a good place to remind students about the language development activities in the digital component which can be assigned for homework.

WRITING An argumentative essay

Ask students to read the information at the top of page 54 so that they know the purpose of the following sections. Make sure they understand what an argumentative essay is.

Background information

An argumentative essay contains at least two different viewpoints which are backed up with supporting evidence. In an argumentative essay, it is important for writers to be clear about which argument they agree with. For example, if the essay is about the advantages and disadvantages of city dwelling, the writer needs to decide if she thinks the advantages outweigh the disadvantages or vice versa.

There are three main structural approaches to the argumentative essay. In all approaches, the writer states the thesis in the introduction. In the first approach, the writer gives the views she agrees with first, then refutes the views that she disagrees with. In the second, she presents and refutes the views that she disagrees with, then presents the ideas she agrees with. In the third, she presents one view she disagrees with, then refutes it, a second view she disagrees with, then refutes it, etc. The final paragraph in all three structures is the conclusion which summarizes the arguments and restates the thesis.

It is important to use good transition words and phrases to move between arguments: *It is believed that …, however, …*. The phrases for expressing contrast learned in Unit 2 will be helpful here.

Writing skill

Introduce the phrase *hedging language* as a synonym for *vague language* or ask students to look up the word *hedging* in their monolingual dictionaries. There are several definitions for hedging, so check that students understand that in this context hedging is avoiding being direct. Some politicians, for example, are very good at hedging. Ask students to read the *Hedging* box to find five ways writers hedge their language.

1 Ask students to underline the hedging language in each sentence, then decide which method from the *Hedging* box is being used.

ANSWERS
1 Generally (adverb of probability) / indicates (verb)
2 appear (verb) / are likely to (adverb of probability)
3 tend to be (verb) / suggests (verb)
4 In some cases (determiner) / may (modal)

Ask students to reflect on how different the sentences would be without the hedging language. Would they be stronger or weaker? (stronger). Ask students why they think it is important to be able to use both types of language.

2 Ask students to read the article and follow the instructions. Put them into pairs to discuss their questions.

ANSWER
The writer presents the information as fact. However, as none of the ideas in the text are supported by empirical evidence, it would be better for the writer to use some hedging language.

SUPPORTING CRITICAL THINKING

Many, many online articles are written in this factual way without any empirical evidence to support the facts. It is easy to read these articles and accept that what is written is true, but good critical thinkers look for evidence which supports reported "facts." Hedging language can make articles more credible because strong claims are avoided.

3 Ask students to rewrite the article, adding hedging language where appropriate. There is no one correct answer, but a possible answer is provided below. Ask students to compare answers.

POSSIBLE ANSWER
A different kind of tourism appears to be helping people to understand how others live. Nicknamed "slum tours," they generally involve trips to the poorest areas and are becoming popular in some cities around the world. Visitors who go on such a tour may learn about the challenges that people who live there face, as well as perhaps discover the positive elements that exist, such as creativity and innovation. Some tour guides employ people from the settlements so the community seems to benefit, and as people become more aware of the life in these communities, they are likely to help more. This tourism is not without controversy, however, as some people believe it could exploit residents of the settlement. They also say that tourists may not be interested in helping residents but may just want to satisfy a curiosity, and that the only people who benefit could be the tour guides.

WRITING TASK

Ask students to read the instructions and refer them to the box with the audience, context, and purpose. Take some time to discuss the writing task with the students to ensure that they understand the essay question (*detrimental* means *harmful* or *damaging*). Point out that they will need to decide where they stand on the issue in order to write their thesis statement, and they might need to cite evidence from the articles on pages 50–51 and 54.

Ask students to read the part of an argumentative essay and follow the instructions. You could also ask students to underline expressions of contrast in a different color *(not only …, but also … On the other hand)*. Ask students to think about whether the writer of this passage is for or against slum tourism (the structure suggests that he is against it).

ANSWERS
The key advantage of slum tourism is thought to be the understanding that tourists gain about the complexities of life in an informal settlement. Visitors can learn not only about the problems that exist within these communities, but also about the supportive community within which the residents live. This could lead to a greater understanding of how society should work together to develop these areas and improve living standards. On the other hand, it is believed that some visitors are not interested in understanding the issues but are instead visiting out of a sense of curiosity. This is unlikely to result in any kind of long-term advantage for the people that agree to be observed, and suggests that these tours are not helpful.

Brainstorm, plan, and write

For the *Brainstorm* section, students can use ideas from the article *City tours, but not as you know them* and their own ideas. Give them some time to work individually, then put them into pairs to generate more ideas from each other. Tell them they need to decide what their opinion is about slum tourism—whether it is positive or detrimental. Ask students to include a thesis statement (a sentence stating their opinion) for good practice.

POSSIBLE ANSWERS

	Advantages	Disadvantages
The tourists	better cultural understanding	—
The residents	work with tour company; tourists may give money to help improve their lives	treated like a tourist attraction, like a zoo; tour companies may not employ local residents; residents are watched by people in expensive clothes with expensive accessories/equipment
The tour company	makes a profit; may help the community; generates cultural understanding	damages their reputation among customers of other products who do not like this venture
Society as a whole	educates people and raises awareness, which can reduce poverty; in long-term, people more motivated to improve living conditions	creates a greater and more obvious social divide

Ask students to create an outline for their essay. Their introduction should contain their thesis statement.

The three middle paragraphs should contain the advantages and drawbacks. The conclusion should briefly summarize the points and re-emphasize the thesis.

You might want to take some time to outline examples of possible structures for the essays on the board, as related to this topic. The example structures here assume that the writer is against slum tourism, but the same structures can be used when the writer is in favor of it.

Structure one

Paragraph 1: thesis: slum tourism is detrimental

Paragraph 2: main idea to support thesis:

- damaging to residents and society
- examples and evidence

Paragraph 3: main idea to support thesis:

- damaging to tour companies
- examples and evidence

Paragraph 4: main idea to refute thesis:

- beneficial to residents and society
- examples and evidence

Conclusion: statement of how the benefits do not outweigh the drawbacks

Structure two

Paragraph 1: thesis: slum tourism is detrimental

Paragraph 2: main idea to refute thesis:

- beneficial to residents and society
- examples and evidence

Paragraph 3: main idea to support thesis:

- damaging to tour companies
- examples and evidence

Paragraph 4: main idea to support thesis

- damaging to residents and society
- examples and evidence

Conclusion: statement of how the benefits do not outweigh the drawbacks

Structure three

Paragraph 1: thesis: slum tourism is detrimental

Paragraph 2:

- how it's beneficial to residents and society
- examples and evidence
- show how, actually, it's negative to residents and society
- examples and evidence

Paragraph 3:

- how it's beneficial to tour companies
- examples and evidence

- show how, actually, it's negative to tour companies
- examples and evidence

Paragraph 4:

- how it's beneficial to tourists
- examples and evidence
- show how, actually, it's negative to tourists
- examples and evidence

Conclusion: statement of how the benefits do not outweigh the drawbacks

The essay excerpt is about 120 words long and is only a single paragraph, but students should aim to write about 300 words. Draw students' attention to the key skills they should demonstrate in their writing: the use of impersonal structures and hedging language, a variety of prepositional phrases. They will also need to use expressions of contrast from Unit 2.

Give students time to write in class, but set a time limit.

Share, rewrite, and edit

Ask students to exchange their essays with a partner. Encourage them to use the Peer review checklist on page 109 when they are evaluating their partner's essay. Try to ensure comments are written down and not just given verbally.

Ask students to rewrite and edit their essays. Encourage them to take into consideration their partner's feedback when rewriting. You could ask students to type and print out the final draft of their essay for homework. You might want to ask them to turn in their first draft, outline, and partner's comments along with their final draft. This will show you how many of the comments they took on board when redrafting. Use the photocopiable *Unit assignment checklist* on page 90 to assess the students' essays. This would also be a good place to ask students to complete the unit checklist in the digital component.

Extra research task

Ask students to research work being done by NGOs in slum areas (search *NGOs in slums* or *NGOs in informal settlements*) to find some of the positive aspects and some of the criticisms of their work. From their research, students should write an argument essay to answer the question: Are NGOs working in slums beneficial or detrimental?

CRITICAL THINKING SKILLS Internal consistency

This section looks closely at creating internal consistency in an argument essay. Internal consistency relates to writing a clear line of argument—something that all writers, whether writing in their native language or not, can struggle to do.

You could lead into the topic by presenting a flawed argument similar to the one on page 56. *Grass is always green. In some places where it is especially hot, the color changes. Grass can be yellow there.* Ask students to identify what is wrong with this argument. Introduce the idea that the argument lacks *internal consistency*. *Consistency* in this context means *coherence, logic*. So, the argument is not logical or coherent.

Ask students to skim-read the three headings on page 56 and write these on the board. These are the three areas related to internal consistency that they will read about, so make sure they understand the terms. *Clarity* means being *clear*. *Opposing* arguments are those that we don't agree with. *Precision* means being *exact* or *accurate*.

Other words from the page that you may wish to pre-teach include: *contradict* (to show that something is not true), *undermine* (to weaken or subvert), *corrode* (destroy chemically), *alternative* (other), *counter argument* (the other side of an argument / opposite viewpoint), *tentative* (careful, cautious).

Ask students to read the first section, *Clarity and internal consistency*, using their monolingual dictionaries if needed. Ask them to discuss how the example contradicts or undermines the main message. Are we sure what point the writer is trying to make? Do we know if he thinks they are good for teeth or not?

Ask students to read the second section, *Including opposing arguments*. Ask them to compare the first example with the second. For each of the points listed, ask students to evaluate the second example—does it follow the four points? Ask students to find and highlight the counter argument, and circle the word that signals the alternative point of view. Ask students to identify tentative, hedging language used by the writer of example 2.

Ask students to read the final section, and discuss the differences between example 3 and example 2. Which starts off more tentatively? (2); Which starts off more strongly? (3). Make sure students understand the final sentence about relative benefits versus the absolute statement. Ask them to underline or highlight the examples of each in example 3.

EXTENSION ACTIVITY

Ask students to look back at their essay to evaluate it for internal consistency. Is there anything they need to change to make a better argument?

Reading	Using headings to understand the main ideas
Critical thinking	Identifying fact, speculation, and opinion
Language development	Words with more than one affix Relative pronouns with prepositions
Writing	Writing definitions

Ask students to look at the picture and say what they think it portrays. Ask questions to stimulate ideas: *Where do you think the man is from? What is he doing? How do you think the picture is related to the unit title, Legacy?*

Background information

The picture shows a Maasai tribesperson using a smartphone. The Maasai people are native to East Africa, living in the Great Rift Valley to the north of Tanzania and the south of Kenya. The Maasai tribe have generally retained their culture and traditions despite the rapid rate of development and modernization in East Africa in recent decades. They are a self-sufficient, semi-nomadic tribe, whose main livelihood comes from livestock, typically cattle, sheep, and goats. The majority of the Maasai still live in extended family groups within traditional *Kraals*. These comprise a circle of mud huts within a protective fence of thorns, which prevents lions and leopards from attacking their livestock at night. Although livestock is the primary currency for the Maasai, many are involved in tourism within the national parks: guiding walking tours, demonstrating their culture and traditions, and selling souvenirs.

Cultural awareness

In the past two decades, language awareness in Western education has become increasingly important. Language is essential to social interaction, which helps us to develop cultural values from an early age. It is also the main way that we exchange cultural and historical information. For these reasons, the benefits of developing an awareness in language learners of the relationship between their mother tongue and the foreign language is now widely recognized. This is said to foster an interest in language and culture, and therefore to facilitate language learning and cultural understanding.

Write *language awareness* and *cultural awareness* on the board, and ask students to discuss the meanings. Read out the *Cultural awareness* text (above) or give students copies to read. Ask them if they agree and how people view language in their culture(s).

Discussion point

As a lead-in, ask the class how many languages they can say "Hello" in. Write the words and their languages on the board (don't worry too much about spelling—if some suggestions are from languages which use symbols, just write the words phonetically).

For questions 2 and 3, students should discuss in pairs or groups of three. Monitor their conversations, encouraging them to give reasons for their answers and to ask follow up questions to extend the discussion. For question 3, after the groups have made their lists, ask them to join with another group to compare ideas and come to a final decision. In the feedback session, ask them to share some of their ideas. Ask: *If everyone in the world spoke the same language, which one should it be? Why?* (The answer need not necessarily be English. Mandarin Chinese has the most speakers as it is the native language of over 10% of the world's population. In addition, China is a growing economic power, and the rest of the world will want to do business with it in future. French and Spanish are also widely spoken throughout the world.) Record any useful vocabulary on the board.

Vocabulary preview

Ask students to work in pairs to read the words in the box. Remind them not to use translators or dictionaries, but to ask others (or you if they are still unsure) for confirmation or clarification of the meanings. Tell them to complete the sentences individually and then compare answers. When going over the answers, ask students to read the full sentences with the words in context. Assist with pronunciation where necessary.

ANSWERS

1 Endangered
2 ethnic groups
3 extinction
4 linguist
5 document
6 tongue
7 revitalize
8 native language

READING Endangered languages: Strategies for preservation and revitalization

Word count 1,008

Before you read

As a lead-in, write the heading, *Endangered languages,* on the board. Check that students understand the meaning of *endangered* and ask: *Why do you think some languages are becoming endangered?* Write some of their ideas on the board and then put them into pairs to discuss the answers. Point out that they should give reasons and explanations for their answers.

ANSWERS
1 7,000 2 40% 3 1%

Global reading

Refer the students to the *Using headings to understand the main ideas* box. After they have read it, ask students: *Does your language use headings in texts? Do you scan headings in your own language? What kind of texts do you do this for? Why is it useful to do this in an exam situation?* (Elicit/Say that it helps you to navigate a text to find the answers you're looking for quickly and efficiently.) Point out that at college or university students will be expected to read and understand large volumes of academic text. It is important that they are able to find relevant information quickly and efficiently to avoid wasting valuable study time. They will also have to use these skills when evaluating the usefulness of research materials.

1 Ask students to read the questions. Check that they understand the meaning of *define* (to describe clearly and exactly what something is) and *extinct* (something that no longer exists). Encourage them to underline the key words in the questions before completing the exercise.

ANSWERS
1 When and why languages become endangered
2 When and why languages become endangered
3 Endangered languages on the rise
4 Revitalization efforts
5 Why endangered languages matter

Exam tip
This exercise practices the skills of skimming and scanning to match paragraph headings, a common task in part 2 of the Academic IELTS Reading Test. In an exam situation, students often feel a sense of panic because they are worried about time constraints and don't take time to skim-read a text before starting on the questions. This can result in poor navigation of the text and inaccurate answers, and ultimately takes much more time. Make a point of practicing these skills consistently throughout the course so that it becomes automatic to your students. Advise them to work on improving their reading speed by practicing skimming and scanning regularly outside class. Broadsheet newspapers are especially useful for this as articles tend to include headings and sub-headings. The text is also organized into columns with each line containing just a few words. This can be helpful in increasing reading speed and confidence before tackling longer, more complex academic or exam texts.

2 Tell students that it is beneficial to skim the whole text quickly before searching for specific answers. Explain that when you skim-read, the brain takes in more information than you first realize. They might be surprised at how quickly they can find information when scanning if they have skim read first. If your students are working towards taking an academic exam such as IELTS, set a time limit of between two and two and a half minutes for them to complete the exercise. Watch students as they read, to see whether they are using the skills and strategies that have been introduced in the book so far—it may be necessary to review some of these with the class for consolidation.

POSSIBLE ANSWERS
1 Languages become endangered due to a number of factors, including globalization, economics, technology, education policy, and changes in cultural attitudes.
2 A language is considered endangered when it has fewer than 1,000 native speakers who make up about half of the language's community; when only some parents speak the language at home; when few of those parents teach the language at home; and when it is not used in schools or for official business.
3 More than 40% of the world's 7,000 languages are endangered (roughly 2,800 languages in total).
4 Efforts to save endangered languages focus on two main areas: the documentation of endangered languages and efforts to increase the use of endangered languages in the community.
5 When a language becomes extinct, oral literature, historical knowledge, and knowledge of the natural world and local environment may all be lost, among other things.

3 If students disagree on any answers, encourage them to revisit the text and point out which part they found them in. Often students guess the answer accurately without fully understanding the text. It is important that they are confident about where they found the answers and why they are correct. Encourage them to get into the habit of annotating the texts (writing the number of the question that is answered beside the correct part of the text) as they complete an exercise or exam task. This allows them to check their answers quickly after finishing.

Draw students' attention to the *Academic keywords* box. Ask students if they know the meaning of the words and teach them if necessary. Review their pronunciation and stress, and tell students to add them to their vocabulary notebooks. If you are following the class wiki project, this unit's wiki group should also add these keywords to the wiki.

Critical thinking skill

SUPPORTING CRITICAL THINKING

Being able to recognize whether a writer is expressing fact, speculation, or opinion is an essential critical thinking skill, especially at advanced levels. Students often have difficulty understanding the differences between these because academic style often sounds factual when in fact it may not be. Cultural factors often play a part in students' ability to identify these features. If they are from an educational background where personal opinion is not valued in academia, they are more likely to assume that the content of an academic text is factual. Some languages do not use modal verbs such as *may*, *might*, *could*, *should* which would help an English speaker to recognize speculation.

A good way to support students with this is to help them develop an awareness of the author's intention. Ask concept questions during lessons and when checking answers, for example, *Is that a fact or an opinion? How do you know? Which words does the writer use to express uncertainty?*

As a lead-in, write *fact*, *speculation*, and *opinion* on the board. Ask students what they mean and how they are different from each other. Ask students if these words translate into their language and if they have the same meaning or a different meaning to the English meanings. Refer them to the *Identifying fact, speculation, and opinion* box and give them a couple of minutes to read it. Afterwards, ask: *Has your idea of the meanings of these words changed? Why do you think it is important to be able to identify these features in a text? How can you identify speculation?*

1 Read through the sentences with the class and check students' understanding of *interrelated* (related in some way), *robust* (strong and successful), and *threat* (a situation or an activity that could cause harm or danger). Ask them to complete the exercise and compare answers with a partner. Encourage them to say why they have chosen fact, opinion, or speculation. Which words helped them to decide? Check answers as a class.

ANSWERS

1 fact	**4** opinion
2 speculation	**5** speculation
3 fact	**6** opinion

2 Remind students that conclusions in academic writing must always be supported by facts or evidence. Ask them to complete exercise 2 individually and then compare answers in pairs or groups of three.

ANSWERS

1 Not supported—Catalogue of Endangered Languages says only about 40% of languages are endangered.
2 Supported—Supporting facts may vary.
3 Not supported—The paper gives examples of languages that have been helped, but does not offer any facts supporting or refuting the idea that these efforts are futile.

Exam tip

In Academic IELTS, it is very important that students are able to identify supporting details. At advanced levels, students should also be able to understand the implications that arise from different types of supporting detail. For example, the statistics given in academic texts are usually facts unless stated otherwise; an expert's opinion is more likely to be correct than the personal opinion of someone who is not a specialist in that subject. An awareness of this can lead to greater accuracy in a *True, False, Not given* reading exam task. To hone these skills, encourage students to regularly discuss the type, source, and wording of supporting details. This helps to improve their critical thinking skills and may also transfer to their own academic writing.

Developing critical thinking

Put students into pairs or small groups for the discussion task. Monitor their discussions and take note of any useful vocabulary or points to expand at the feedback stage.

SUPPORTING CRITICAL THINKING

The questions in this section require the students to evaluate and give opinions on some of the points raised in the text. In question 2, they are required to consider the wider implications of the loss of a language. Being able to see the big picture in any situation is a key critical thinking skill which demonstrates depth of understanding. Ask students to compile a list of effects before discussing which makes the strongest argument. They should then compare their ideas with another group, giving reasons and supporting details for their choices.

EXTENSION ACTIVITY

If class opinion on the effect of technology on languages is divided, organize a class debate. Confident classes could do this immediately, or you may wish to do this in a subsequent lesson to give students time to research their arguments in more detail.

Before the debate, divide students into groups and give them time to plan their arguments. Encourage them to support their arguments with facts. Tell students to listen carefully to the opposing team while the debate is in progress and take notes so that they can counteract their arguments logically. Explain that a debate is a two-way situation and it's important to avoid a situation where both teams are arguing their points without interacting with each other. As a further challenge for competent classes, establish student opinion and then ask them to argue for the opposite of it. This helps improve critical thinking skills as students have to work harder to see the situation from the opposite perspective.

Language development: Words with more than one affix

Background information

Affixes are particularly common in academic vocabulary. This is because it is mainly derived from Latin, which used affixes as a system for building words around a base or "root."

Prefixes: *Pre* means *before*, so a prefix is added before the root, i.e., prefix *en* + root *danger* = *endanger*. The meaning of prefixes can be grammatical to show word class, e.g., *re* (do something again) which makes verbs such as *revitalize, reassess*. They often form antonyms, i.e., prefix *im* + root *possible* = *impossible*. They also express particular meanings, e.g., *bio* (of living things) = *biography, biosciences*.

Suffixes: *Suf* means *after*, and therefore a suffix is positioned after the root at the end of a word, i.e., root *valid* + suffix *ate* = *validate*. Suffixes generally change word class, for example, *manage* is a verb, but *management* is a noun.

Elicit/Explain that understanding the function and meaning of affixes can greatly assist students in building their vocabulary quickly. It also develops their autonomy because if they understand the meaning of an affix, they are more likely to be able to work out the meaning of new words in an academic context without having to rely heavily on their dictionaries.

1 Ask students to complete exercise 1 individually or in pairs. Point out that all the words required to complete the sentences can be found in the text. Allow monolingual dictionary use if necessary, but encourage students to ask their classmates first. When going over the answers, ask students to read the full sentences with the word in context and practice pronouncing the words correctly as a class. Encourage students to make a note of the new words in their vocabulary notebooks and suggest that they write sentences with the words in context during independent study.

ANSWERS

1 revitalize
2 popularization (NB: popularity also fits grammatically, but the rubric states that 2+ affixes must be added.)
3 endangerment
4 Globalization
5 validation
6 revitalization
7 disappearance
8 classification

2 Ask students to discuss their opinions in pairs or small groups. Set a time limit of approximately five minutes for the speaking part of this task to avoid students immediately starting on writing their sentences. Point out that this is a good opportunity for them to practice using words with affixes in context. Encourage them to give reasons and examples and to ask follow-up questions during their discussion. Monitor while students have their discussions, and take note of any useful points to raise or review at the feedback stage. When students have finished writing their sentences, give them some time to compare and peer correct before feeding back.

This is a good place to use the video resource *Tracing the family line*. It is located in the Video resources section of the digital component. Alternatively, remind students about the video so they can do this at home. If you are following the class wiki project, this unit's wiki group should also add these keywords to the wiki.

EXTENSION ACTIVITY

Students often have difficulties with the pronunciation and rhythm of long academic words, particularly those with affixes. Tell students that at advanced levels they will need to use advanced vocabulary in speaking exams, tutorial discussions, and when giving presentations. Explain that there is a pronunciation rule for words ending in the suffix *-tion*. Write on the board the word *classify* and tap or clap the rhythm Ooo. Ask students to copy you and then say *classify* in this rhythm. Ask: *Which syllable is stressed?* (the first). Next, write *classification*, again tap or clap the rhythm oooOo, and get students to copy and say *classification*. Ask students: *Is the stress still on the first syllable?* (no); *How many syllables are there in classification?* (five); *Which syllable is stressed?* (the fourth syllable *ca* before the suffix *-tion*). Write *generalization* on the board and ask students how to pronounce it. Elicit/Explain that it has the same rhythm as *classification*—words are usually stressed on the syllable before the suffix *-tion*.

Ask students to work in pairs to test each other, i.e., Student A says <u>glo</u>bal, and Student B says *globali<u>za</u>tion*. Encourage them to tap or clap the rhythm if they are having difficulty. If they are doing well, you could ask them to add an example sentence with the word in context. Suggest that they record words in groups according to their stress patterns, for example, using headings such as oooOo.

Language development: Relative pronouns with prepositions

Students may have come across the use of relative pronouns with prepositions before in the course of their study, but they are unlikely to be using such a sophisticated structure themselves. The use of prepositions before pronouns in English is considered good academic style, and students should try to emulate this at more advanced levels. However, prepositions themselves, and their position, are often a source of confusion, particularly if students are from a culture which does not use them, or uses them in a different way. For consolidation, try to review this structure regularly in subsequent lessons, and praise students when they use it correctly when writing.

Give students plenty of time to study the examples in the *Relative pronouns with prepositions* box and ask any necessary questions. Direct their attention to the paragraph, set a time limit of 30 seconds, and ask them to skim-read it and then tell you the gist of the topic (it describes the situation of an endangered language in South America). Students should then work individually to complete the paragraph before comparing answers with a partner.

ANSWERS

1 of which	**5** in which
2 in which	**6** of which
3 of which	**7** for which
4 with whom	**8** in which

WRITING Describing changes

Background information

Definitions are an integral part of academic writing where scientific or technical terms are commonly used. Students within an academic context will be expected to show knowledge and understanding of key subject-related terms, and be able to define them clearly for a reader or listener who does not necessarily have specialist knowledge.

As a lead-in, ask students to think of a custom or tradition in their country that has become less common and think of at least two reasons for this. Give them a minute or two to write brief notes before discussing with a partner. Afterwards, ask students to feed back some of their partner's answers. Write any useful words and phrases on the board.

Writing skill

Ask students to read the *Writing definitions* box and ask you any necessary questions. It is worth pointing out that *refer to* is generally considered more academic and formal than *is called*, however it is important to vary language when writing, rather than repeating the same phrases throughout an assignment.

1 Do the first sentence on the board as an example. Ask students to choose language from the *Writing definitions* box to construct it. Write their suggestions on the board. Example sentence: *Pisan zapra is a Malay term/word which refers to / means the length of time needed to eat a banana*. Ask students to complete the rest of the exercise individually, but allow them to discuss ideas if it helps. Give them time to compare answers, evaluate, and peer correct afterwards.

POSSIBLE ANSWERS

1 *Pisan zapra* is a Malay word that refers to the length of time needed to eat a banana.
2 The act of tiptoeing over warm sand is called *hanyauku* in the Kwangali language.
3 The Scottish word *tartle* is defined as "to hesitate while introducing a person because you can't remember his/her name."
4 A joke that is so unfunny and badly told that a person can't help but laugh is referred to as a *jayus* in the Indonesian language.
5 *Mokita* is a word in the Kilivila language that means something we all know but agree not to talk about.
6 In the Rapa Nui language, *tingo* is a term for stealing all of your neighbor's possessions by gradually borrowing them one by one.

2 Students may wish to write their definitions in pairs, before comparing answers in groups. Ask them to feed back some of their definitions, and do error correction on the board where necessary.

EXTENSION ACTIVITY

Play the "Dictionary Game." Divide students into groups of three. Ask them to choose a word from the dictionary that they think their classmates will not know (preferably this will be an academic term, but you may decide otherwise if you think the students may find this too challenging). They should read this and then work together to write <u>one</u> *true* definition and <u>two</u> *false* definitions. Encourage students to make their false definitions as plausible as possible and to use academic style. When all the groups are ready, they take turns to read their definitions to the class, and the groups guess which of the three definitions is true. Make it a competition—award two points for a correct answer. The team with the most points wins.

WRITING TASK

Background information

Critical analysis is a key process in university study. It involves analyzing information, evaluating it, and comparing it against other data; categorizing; finding connections; questioning; making judgements and forming opinions while reading an academic text; writing an assignment; listening to a lecture; speaking in a tutorial; or giving a presentation. It is an active thinking process where students are required to respond to, question, and expand concepts rather than passively accepting the information that is presented to them.

Refer students to the box at the top of the page which outlines the audience, context, and purpose. Elicit/Explain the meaning of *critical analysis* (see the *Background information* box above). Ask them to read the data and then discuss the question in pairs. Give them a time limit of five to seven minutes. Point out that this is an opportunity to practice supporting their opinions with facts from the text (a skill practiced earlier in the unit).

Brainstorm, plan, and write

Ask students to read the data and discuss the questions. Suggest that they make notes to compare the languages such as in a mind map format (this often helps the more visual learners to organize their thoughts).

Remind students that they should always make a plan before writing. Ask them to work individually to note the two reasons for their choice, and then evaluate them in pairs. Emphasize that these reasons will form the topics for each of the two body paragraphs. Encourage students to discuss and evaluate their plans before moving on to the writing stage. Ask students to write a plan including ideas and support for the introduction, two paragraphs, and the conclusion. Give the students a time limit of ten minutes to write their plan.

Ideally, class time could be given for the writing task so that you can monitor and assist students where necessary. Tell students that their essays should be approximately 300 words long. Remind them of the audience, context, and purpose of their essay, and set a time limit of approximately ten minutes for planning, and then 40–60 minutes for the first draft.

Share, rewrite, and edit

Ask students to exchange their essays with a partner. Encourage them to use the Peer review checklist on page 109 when they are evaluating their partner's essays. Remind students that this stage is very beneficial to them so they should take their role as evaluator seriously. They should use the checklist to make constructive comments on their partner's essay. Give them a time limit of around ten minutes. Encourage them to number the parts of the essay that they want to comment on and then take notes corresponding to these numbers on a separate piece of paper to share with their partner as they give spoken feedback. The student whose work is being analyzed should respond by accepting, rejecting, or asking for further explanation and clarification. They can then write their own comments (based on the feedback and resulting decisions) on their essay to help them when they rewrite.

Ask students to rewrite and edit their essays. Encourage them to take into consideration their partner's feedback when rewriting. Encourage students to discuss any necessary improvements in detail and attempt to think about how they could improve their level and accuracy next time around. Ask students to rewrite the essay for homework. Use the photocopiable *Unit assignment checklist* on page 91 to assess the students' essays.

Extra research task

This task could be done as a presentation to the class, a group, or if students are preparing for the IELTS Speaking Test, a long turn. Ask students to research and prepare a short presentation. They should speak for approximately two minutes about one of the following topics:

- An endangered language (where it is spoken and by whom, how it is being revitalized)
- The effect of technology on languages
- The importance of language to traditional culture
- Other (if students have a specific topic-related presentation in mind, ask them to check with you first before researching).

On the day of the presentations, allow students plenty of planning and practice time. To keep students in the audience listening, ask them to take notes so that they could summarize the main points afterwards, or to write at least two relevant questions to ask at the end of each presentation.

STUDY SKILLS Academic referencing

Cultural awareness

As mentioned in Unit 3, plagiarism is a serious offence in Western academia. However, it is important to recognize that students may not take care to reference thoroughly because they do not always consider plagiarism as cheating. Copying a known intellectual author is acceptable, and even encouraged, in some education systems. To avoid offending your students' formative education, it is advisable to explain how plagiarism is viewed negatively in Western cultures where an individual's intellectual property is protected by law, rather than suggesting it is simply "wrong." It is also worth explaining that referencing is a way for tutors and professors to find the sources students have used in their writing if they want to. It is important to regularly check that they are confident about how to reference from a range of sources including essays, journals, books, websites, or blogs. Point out that whatever the source, it must always be referenced. Many students don't realize that articles and images taken from the Internet should also be referenced despite being in the public domain.

Getting started

Refer students to the title *Academic referencing*, and ask them what they know about it. Put them into pairs to discuss the meanings of the words in the box. Encourage students to ask each other the meanings before checking in their monolingual dictionaries. Check their understanding and review their pronunciation before asking students to move on to questions 2 and 3. When they have finished, ask them to feed back the answers they discussed. Find out if they think there are any differences between academic referencing in English and in their own language.

ANSWERS

1 bibliography: a list of the books, articles, etc. that someone has used for finding information for a piece of work they have written
citation: a phrase or sentence taken from a piece of writing or speech
credits: acknowledgement for something you have done or achieved
index: an alphabetical list of something such as subjects or names at the back of a book that shows on which page they are mentioned
reference (list): a writer or a piece of work that is mentioned in a piece of writing by someone else
2 family name of the author and date of publication
3 authors, date, title of academic paper, conference details, page numbers
authors, date, title of academic paper, full URL, date accessed

Scenario

Refer students to the picture of Julia. Ask them to skim-read the scenario, and then briefly discuss the gist with them. Ask them to read the scenario again and follow the instructions. Give them some time to think about the answer to the question, and then put them in pairs to discuss it. In the feedback session, write some of the students' ideas on the board.

POSSIBLE ANSWERS

Julia sounds like she is a dedicated student; taking notes, summarizing, and paraphrasing. She is also careful to list source references. However, she is not having so much success with her term papers or essays as compared to previously. There is something different in her transition from engineering to psychology. These subjects are very different, with one being math based and the other social science based. It may well be that she is not adapting to the change in style of writing needed for psychology. Another factor could be simply that her tutor grades more harshly. There could also be another factor to do with essay styles, as hinted by the mention of source references.

EXTENSION ACTIVITY

Refer students to the end of the *Endangered languages* text on page 61. Ask them to read through the sources and 1) note which information is included, and 2) note the different types of source material, i.e., newspaper (*Guardian*: leading broadsheet newspaper in the U.K.); catalogue (Catalogue of Endangered Languages); website/blog (Endangered Languages Project); scientific monthly publication (*National Geographic*); radio (National Public Radio: explain to students that many radio broadcasters provide an archive of radio transcripts to read, and podcasts to listen to online. They can use these as a valuable resource for information, study, and listening practice.).

Consider it

Ask students to read the instructions and discuss the questions. If they have not heard of the style guides mentioned, suggest that they look them up online by typing their titles into an Internet search engine.

Over to you

Provide some authentic academic texts for students to look at in class. Try to include a range of formats including essays, reports, journals, and books on a variety of academic subjects. Ask students to work in pairs to compare and discuss the referencing styles used in each. Discuss the final question (if relevant to your students) as a class. Elicit/Emphasize that different institutions and subjects have their own preferred referencing style. It is vital that students check with their tutor on their course which style or styles of referencing are acceptable, or consult the course handbook. Ask students to include accurate referencing in their next writing assignment.

UNIT 7 EXPANSE

Reading	Identifying persuasion techniques
Critical thinking	Assessing the logic of an argument
Language development	Adjective + noun collocations Noun (nominal) clauses
Writing	Emphasizing your point

Ask students to look at the picture and describe what they see. Ask questions to stimulate ideas: *How do you feel when you see images of the Earth?* (Students may find them fascinating or even unnerving due to the magnitude of unexplored space.); *How do you think the picture is related to the unit title, Expanse?*

Discussion point

As a lead-in, you could do a brief quiz with information from the *Background information* box below. Divide the students into pairs or groups of three, ask each question, and give them time to discuss their answers before responding. Ask: *How many people live in China? a) 1.1 billion, b) 1.25 billion, or 1.4 billion?* (1.4 billion); *Which country has the second largest population? a) the United States, b) India, c) Canada?* (India); *What percentage of the world's population do you think is between 14 and 44 years old? a) 25%, b) 7.9%, or c) 45%?* (45%); *Who generally lives longer, men or women?* (women).

Background information

The Earth has a population of approximately seven billion, which is estimated to be increasing by over 1% per year. The most populated country in the world is China, which is home to around 1.4 billion people, followed by India with over 1.25 billion. Statistics show that the majority of the world's population is young—over 45% of people are aged between 15 and 44 years old, and more than 25% are 14 and under. Although a relatively small percentage of people are over 65 (an estimated 7.9%), within the last 40 years life expectancy has increased worldwide by approximately 11 years for men and 12 years for women. Experts believe that this trend is set to continue.

Sources (accessed July 2013):
http://www.worldometers.info/world-population/
http://worldpollutionfacts.com/2013/04/world-population-facts/

http://www.geohive.com/earth/population_age_1.aspx

http://www.guardian.co.uk/society/2012/dec/13/life-expectancy-world-rise

If students have done the quiz, they should remain in their pairs or groups of three to discuss the questions. Monitor their conversations without interrupting and take note of any points to feed back on afterwards.

For question 2, tell students to complete their ranking individually before comparing with their partner or partners in question 3.

Set a time limit of around eight minutes for question 3. Point out that the process of ranking and rating gives them a valuable opportunity to express their opinions, giving reasons, examples, and explanations. Remind them that this unit will look at persuasion techniques in more detail later, so they should try to persuade the other members of their group of their opinions. However, reaching a *consensus* (coming to an agreement) on the two main issues is the desired outcome, so they should try to achieve this. Ask groups to feed back on their two main issues. Write any useful topic-related vocabulary on the board.

EXTENSION ACTIVITY

Extend the discussion in question 3 to try to reach a class consensus. Groups are likely to have chosen different main issues. Ask pairs/groups of three to prepare a brief presentation of one or two minutes to the class. Give them time to prepare, and tell them to give at least *two* persuasive reasons for each choice and support these with facts and examples if possible. After all the pairs/groups have made their presentations, ask the class to try to come to a consensus. Encourage them to comment on each other's presentations, i.e., *Tao, I liked the points you raised about global warming. That's a valid point, but I'm afraid I disagree because ...* If time is limited, this activity could be set for homework.

Vocabulary preview

Remind students to try to guess the meanings from the context. Ask them to think about the meanings of the words individually and then compare answers with a partner. Assist with pronunciation and clarification of meanings where necessary.

ANSWERS

1 there is not much of something
2 placing pressure on
3 using a part of something
4 energy sources that are replaced naturally and never used up
5 methods that do not harm the environment
6 a large area of buildings, etc., that have spread from a city into the countryside, usually in an unattractive way

7 bring water to land to grow crops
8 ceased to exist
9 the process by which earth is removed by rain, wind, or the sea
10 very successful
11 the variety of different types of plants and animals that live in a region
12 a situation that is the worst you can imagine

READING Overpopulation: A problem or a myth?

Word count 1,198

Before you read

As a lead-in, write *Overpopulation: A problem or a myth?* on the board. Check that students understand the meaning of *myth* and ask: *Why do you think the writer has introduced the possibility that overpopulation may not occur?* Elicit/Explain that maybe some people believe that there are solutions to avoid overpopulation, for example, through sustainability and the use of renewable energy.

Put students into pairs to discuss the question. Point out that this is a good opportunity to exercise their critical thinking skills. Suggest that they brainstorm lists of the benefits and problems, and then join another pair to compare lists in groups. Monitor the discussions and take note of any interesting points or vocabulary raised to highlight at the feedback stage afterwards.

Global reading

Refer the students to the *Identifying persuasion techniques* box. After they have read it, ask them to recap the main points by asking: *What techniques does a writer of an academic text use to persuade the reader to agree with them? What techniques are used by writers of informal texts? Do writers use any of these techniques in your native language?* Explain that these techniques can also be used in presentations and seminars, and when debating.

1 Elicit / Point out that this text is divided into two sections giving different perspectives on population growth. These are labelled *A problem* and *A myth*, and each one is written by a different author. Draw their attention to the *Academic keywords* box. Ask if they know the meaning of the words and explain them if necessary. Review their pronunciation and stress, and ask students to add them to their vocabulary notebooks. If you are following the class wiki project, this unit's wiki group should also add these keywords to the wiki. Give students a time limit of a couple of minutes to skim-read the text, and then briefly discuss the gist in open class before asking them to re-read it in more detail. Explain that they will need to refer to the supporting reasons in exercises 2 and 3, so they should underline them in the text so that they can find them again quickly.

2 Remind students that it is beneficial to underline key words or phrases that they want to find to help them focus when skimming and scanning in the text. Again, suggest that they underline and mark them with a number or letter for quick reference.

Exam tip

This exercise requires students to use skimming and scanning skills, which are vital for success in the Academic IELTS Reading Test, particularly in tasks about identifying the writer's views such as *True, False, Not given* and multiple choice questions. As mentioned in Unit 6, it is important that students get into the habit of practicing these skills regularly. In addition, they should consistently underline and label their texts with question numbers in order to allow for quick and effective checking after completing the test.

ANSWERS

Argument A: A problem

Repetition for emphasis Paragraph 1: the same number of people who currently live in the African and American continents combined

Future insights Paragraph 2: That is more than twice the number of people we have today.
Paragraph 3: Without clean drinking water, there will be a rapid rise in diseases … / This is likely to increase …
Paragraph 5: It is therefore likely that there will be a higher demand for oil … / This will make it more difficult …

Questions Paragraph 4: How can we allow this destruction to occur under our noses …?
Paragraph 6: Who can argue with free and equal education for everyone?

Argument B: A myth

Repetition for emphasis Paragraph 4: … which means that a fifth of us use four-fifths of the world's food and energy.

Future insights Paragraph 2: … it is the low variant that has come true in the past … suggesting the same will be true of their future population predictions.
Paragraph 5: … we may find ourselves living on a planet that can no longer sustain human life.

Dismissing alternative arguments Paragraph 3: … Raj Krishna estimates that India alone is capable of increasing crop yields to the point of providing the entire world's food supply. / There is the same amount of fresh water on the planet now as there was 10,000 years ago.

Emotional vocabulary Paragraph 4: sad truth; Paragraph 5: horrendous.

3 Put students into pairs or groups of three to discuss their opinions. Encourage them to give reasons, referring to the persuasion techniques in the *Identifying persuasion techniques* box where necessary.

Critical thinking skill

SUPPORTING CRITICAL THINKING

At a Western college or university, students will be expected to be able to assess the logic of a writer's arguments and comment on them. They are likely to find this challenging at first, particularly if they haven't been used to doing this in their native education system. These skills will take time to build, so encourage your students to give their opinions as much as possible in lessons and ask questions such as *Do you think this is a logical argument? Is this a valid point? Why or why not?*

As a lead-in, write *logical* on the board and ask students what it means. Then ask: *Are a writer's arguments always logical? Why is it important to be able to assess the logic of the arguments in a text?* Write some of their ideas on the board and then refer them to the *Assessing the logic of an argument* box. Give them time to read it, and then ask if it mentions any of their earlier suggestions and ask them to recap the general points.

1 Remind students to circle or underline the statistics in the text for quick reference. Ask them to complete exercise 1 and compare answers with a partner. Encourage them to give reasons and explanations if they disagree on any.

ANSWERS

a trend
b static figure
c static figure
d pattern
e static figure
f trend

2 Ask students to stay in pairs to discuss question 2.

POSSIBLE ANSWER

Dr. Rice is illustrating that the problem of overpopulation is increasing / getting worse.

Exam tip

In Academic IELTS Writing Task 2, students may have to write an argument-led essay. In this style of essay, they are required to present the arguments for and against a topic, and then give their own opinion. They will need to give reasons why they disagree with the opposing arguments. Point out that the skills practiced in this lesson are extremely important for this type of task. Remind them that all skills are transferable to other disciplines, for example, recognizing arguments when reading, and then assessing them through discussion, which may also lead to them using these critical assessment skills naturally and confidently when writing.

3 Read through the sentences with the students and check the meaning of any potentially new vocabulary such as *deforestation, overconsumption,* and *occurrence*. Point out that all three words demonstrate the use of affixes for word building which was introduced in Unit 6. Encourage students to work out the meanings from the root of the words (i.e., *forest, consume,* and *occur*). Elicit / Point out that the suffix *-tion* often describes a *process*.

ANSWERS

A problem
1 no (even though the text suggests this, the use of *will* is too strong)
2 no (even though the text suggests this, the use of *will* is too strong)
3 yes (there is evidence of the negative effects of deforestation and mining)
4 yes (statistics support it)
5 yes and no (education is likely to be one of a number of solutions)

A myth
6 no (if there is a finite amount of water, then logically a higher population will put more strain on this amount)
7 no (this is a generalization which is unlikely)
8 yes (we can see plenty of evidence of waste, and there will be statistics available)
9 no (even though the text suggests this, the use of *will* is too strong)
10 no (even though the text suggests this, the use of *will* is too strong)

4 Ask students to form small groups to discuss their ideas, and then decide which writer gave the most logical arguments. Monitor and take note on any points to feed back on at the end. During the feedback session, make the emphasis on improving critical thinking and expanding ideas rather than grammatical errors. Remember to say what students did well as well as suggesting how they can improve.

POSSIBLE ANSWER

Dr. Rice has the better and more logical arguments as they are supported by evidence; the research is valid and reliable, and supports the conclusions. Marilyn Cratchley's text is not a good academic model. She does not support her arguments with effective points, and they do not all support the conclusions.

Developing critical thinking

SUPPORTING CRITICAL THINKING

The questions in this section require the students to offer solutions to the potential problems raised in the text. In question 2, they consider solutions to the problem of overconsumption across a range of groups throughout society. Suggest that they brainstorm ideas in small groups using mind maps. Demonstrate this on the board with the headwords: *individuals, schools, governments, business leaders*, and ask students to suggest a few example solutions. Ask them to copy the mind maps into their notebooks and complete them in groups. Point out that organizing their notes in a way that helps them to think clearly when speaking or writing is a highly useful skill. They should then compare their ideas with another group, giving reasons and supporting details for their choices.

Put students into pairs or small groups for the discussion. Give them a couple of minutes to prepare their suggestions before having the discussion. Monitor their discussions unobtrusively and take note of any useful vocabulary or points to expand at the feedback stage.

EXTENSION ACTIVITY

Put students into pairs and ask them to choose one of the groups from question 2, for example, business leaders. Ask them to prepare a short presentation (approximately two minutes long) outlining three things that they are going to do to try to reduce the problem of overconsumption. They should give reasons and examples for each. Give them time to prepare and practice their presentations. Tell the class that they should listen carefully and decide who gave the best solutions. Have a class vote at the end.

Language development: Adjective + noun collocations

Ask students to read the *Adjective + noun collocations* box and check that they understand the content. At advanced levels, having a wide vocabulary is essential, but it is not enough just to know the meanings of academic words; it is also important to know how they work together. Students can increase their vocabulary and accuracy by learning collocations. A good way to remember them is to record them in categories in their vocabulary notebooks.

1 Ask students to complete exercise 1 individually or in pairs. When going over the answers, ask students to read the full sentences with the word in context. Practice pronouncing the words correctly as a class and encourage students to write any new collocations in their vocabulary notebooks. Remind them to write sentences with the words in context during independent study.

ANSWERS

1 enormous	6 prime
2 profound	7 huge
3 major	8 greater
4 rapid	9 higher
5 greater	10 bigger

2 Ask students to complete the sentences individually and then return to their pairs to compare answers. Check answers as a class, getting students to say the whole sentence with the answers in context for fluency practice.

ANSWERS

1 **a** considerable **b** widespread **c** systematic
2 **a** substantial **b** crucial **c** prominent
3 **a** principal **b** acute **c** leading

This is a good place to use the video resource *Infinite boundaries*. It is located in the Video resources section of the digital component. Alternatively, remind students about the video so they can do this at home. If you are following the class wiki project, this unit's wiki group should also add these keywords to the wiki.

EXTENSION ACTIVITY

Put students into groups of three or four. Ask them to discuss the statements in exercise 2, expanding them with reasons and examples. Point out that this is a good opportunity for them to use the adjective + noun collocations that they have just practiced, as well as the skills of persuasion from the unit so far.

3 Set a time limit of a few minutes for students to brainstorm their three issues and the reasons why people are concerned about them in pairs. Ask them to write their sentences individually, referring back to exercises 1 and 2 where necessary. Ask them to compare sentences with their partner and peer correct. Afterwards, write some of their example sentences on the board for the class to copy.

Language development: Noun (nominal) clauses

Give students plenty of time to study the examples in the *Noun (nominal) clauses* box and ask any questions they may have. It is likely that they haven't studied noun clauses in detail before. They can be very complex, so students may need extra support and practice with these exercises. Explain that noun clauses make up around two thirds of an academic text, and that recognizing how they are used can help them to understand complex texts and to develop a more academic writing style for themselves.

Background information

Most education systems place great importance on the verb in English language teaching, and as a result students tend to overuse verb phrases in production. Approximately two thirds of an academic text consists of noun clauses. This can disadvantage even very advanced students at university as they appear to have an immature, less academic writing or presentation style. At high levels, students will come across noun clauses when reading. These can be long and complicated because they contain a lot of information, and understanding them better will help students' general reading comprehension. More advanced students may be able to understand complex noun clauses, but they may not have considered why and how they are used in any detail. One way to help your students to begin using noun clauses themselves is to encourage them to notice how they are used in academic and informational texts such as textbooks and journals. Explain that as their level of English improves, they should try to notice the distribution of verbs and nouns in the texts they study, and attempt to mirror this in their own writing. An activity which may help to raise your students' awareness of how nouns are used in texts is included in the *Extension activity* box at the end of this section.

1 Allow students to work with a partner to do the exercise if they wish. Ask them to compare answers afterwards with another student or pair. Point out that they can study how noun clauses are used in texts during independent study in the same way—underlining or circling text, and noticing which types of clauses are used and how often.

ANSWERS
1 they can follow fashion without spending much money
2 that fast fashion affects the environment
3 that polyester is made from petroleum
4 What may result from this
5 How cotton is grown
6 whether they need new clothes or not

2 Ask students to complete the sentences and then compare answers with a partner.

ANSWERS

1 that	4 that
2 that	5 What
3 How/Where	6 if/whether

3 Put students into new pairs, or small groups. Give them a few minutes to re-read the statements, reflect, and take notes before beginning the discussion. Point out that this is a good opportunity for them to try using noun clauses as they speak. Monitor during the discussions and take note of any interesting points or good examples of noun clauses to share with the class afterwards.

EXTENSION ACTIVITY

As mentioned in the *Background information* box, academic texts tend to use a much higher proportion of nouns and noun clauses than informal texts. To demonstrate this, photocopy two texts—one academic and one informal—from a blog or lifestyle magazine (if possible, use texts covering the same topic or story). Put students into pairs and ask them to work together to circle all the nouns in the texts and then compare the differences. Afterwards, ask them to try to translate the informal text into an academic one using noun clauses where possible.

WRITING A persuasive essay

Cultural awareness

This essay type is likely to present challenges for students from educational backgrounds where personal opinion is not considered relevant within an academic context. The exercises in this section will help students by building the skills and confidence they need to be persuasive in putting forward their opinions—something that they will need consistent practice and support with from you throughout their course of study.

As a lead-in, ask students to think of some situations where you may need to be persuasive (i.e., in interviews, assignments, debates and tutorial groups, in a professional setting at meetings, and when making important business decisions). Write some of the students' ideas on the board.

Writing skill

Ask students to read the *Emphasizing your point* box and ask you any questions they may have.

Background information

The *Emphasizing your point* box presents examples of emphasis. For consolidation and further clarification, explain the following point:
Sentences starting with preparatory *It* are usually used with a *that* clause, as in the example, or a relative pronoun.
It is the company director who is responsible for the poor morale of the staff.
It is our children whose future will be affected by the environmental damage we cause.

1 Do the first sentence on the board with the class as an example. Invite students to attempt to rephrase it (*Only when humans started to grow crops and keep farm animals did world population begin to increase more quickly.*). Write their suggestions on the board. Elicit / Point out that the auxiliary verb *did* is required at the beginning of the second clause after the adverb *only*. Ask students to complete the rest of the exercise individually, but allow them to

discuss ideas with a partner if they wish. Give them time to compare answers, evaluate, and peer correct before checking answers as a class. If necessary, write the full answers on the board to clarify.

ANSWERS

1 Only when humans started to grow crops and keep farm animals did the world population begin to increase more quickly.
2 What many people do not realize is that our world cannot continue to sustain our needs.
3 Rarely do world leaders discuss the issue of overpopulation.
4 It is governments that should address the issue of world poverty. / It is the issue of world poverty that governments should address.
5 Not only does education help people escape poverty, it also helps them understand global issues.
6 It is men who are more likely to be educated than women.
7 It is now that we should address these issues and not in the future.

2 Ask students: *What is literacy?* (the ability to read and write). Put students into pairs to discuss the question. When they are finished, ask some students to report some of their ideas to the class. Write any useful topic-related vocabulary and phrases on the board.

3 Ask the students to scan the article to find the opposite of *literacy* (*illiteracy*). Give them a minute or two to read the article and then discuss whether it mentioned any of their ideas. Briefly recap the contents of the article before moving on to exercise 4.

4 Suggest that students attempt this exercise individually and then compare sentences with a partner.

ANSWERS

1 it is the ability to read and write that affects your life the most
2 Rarely do you
3 it does make
4 What you have to do is rely on other people
5 Not only does illiteracy affect a person individually, (but) it also reduces

EXTENSION ACTIVITY

Ask students to find a short text (a journal or newspaper article) of their own in independent study time and bring it to the next lesson. Ask them to read it and write six to eight sentences about it using the inversion techniques from the lesson. Ideally, this should be done in class so that you can support students and assist where necessary. Confident students could do this activity for homework and peer evaluate in pairs in the next lesson.

WRITING TASK

As a lead-in, write on the board: *Describe your country's education system. How old are you when you start? How many people are there in an average class? Which subjects do you study? Are the classes teacher-focused or student-focused? How do you think this system could be improved?* Note: *Teacher-focused* is where the teacher talks and students listen, and *student-focused* is where the students are encouraged to work in pairs or groups and contribute verbally to lessons. Give students a few minutes to discuss the questions in pairs. Monitor and listen for any interesting points to discuss when the students feed back some of their partners' answers.

Refer students to the box at the top of the page which outlines the audience, context, and purpose. Ask them to read the instructions and then briefly tell you what the task requires them to do (write a persuasive essay on behalf of an international charity).

Ask students to read the introduction in detail and then do the exercise individually. When they have finished, ask them to compare answers with a partner before checking answers as a class.

ANSWERS

1 P 2 A 3 E 4 A 5 A 6 A

Brainstorm, plan, and write

Ask students to read through the notes. Suggest that they copy them onto a separate piece of paper so that they have space to add to them. Ask them to work individually for a minute or two and then in pairs to expand their ideas. Ask students to feed back some of their notes to the class before moving on to the planning stage.

Remind students that they should always have a clear plan to refer to when writing. Point out that reasons 1–3 will form the topics for each of the body paragraphs. Ask them to work individually to complete their plans, and then evaluate them with their partner.

POSSIBLE ANSWER

Possible reasons to support free and equal education for all:
Reason 1: Improves people's health as they understand how to look after themselves and perhaps feel they have more to live for. This is passed on to children, and slowly, poor health due to poverty is eradicated. Also, family sizes are known to reduce.
Reason 2: Improves personal economic situation. People who are literate and educated can look for work that is better paid (and also less dangerous or physically demanding) and provide better for their families.
Reason 3: Improves economic situation. Countries develop greater GDP per capita and can produce more economically with the resources they have.

Conclusion: However, in practice it is difficult to provide education for all, and it is possible for health and poverty to impact on whether a child goes to school or not. Therefore, there is the opposite correlation.

Ideally, the writing task should be done in class time so that you can monitor and assist students if necessary. Tell them that their essays should be approximately 300 words long. Remind them of the audience, context, and purpose of their essay, and set a time limit of approximately 40 minutes. Emphasize that this is a good opportunity for them to include adjective + noun collocations and noun clauses in their writing while it is still fresh in their minds.

Share, rewrite, and edit

Ask students to exchange their essays with a partner. Encourage them to use the Peer review checklist on page 109 when they are evaluating their partner's essays. Remind students that this stage is very beneficial to them so they should take their role as evaluator seriously. Explain that they should use the checklist to make constructive comments on their partner's essay. Give them a time limit of around ten minutes. Encourage them to number the parts of the essay that they want to comment on and then take notes corresponding to these numbers on a separate piece of paper to refer to as they give feedback. Remind them also to say what their partner did well.

Ask students to rewrite and edit their essays. Encourage them to take into consideration their partner's feedback when rewriting. Encourage students to discuss suggested improvements in detail and attempt to think about how they rewrite with greater accuracy next time around. Ask students to rewrite the essay for homework. Use the photocopiable *Unit assignment checklist* on page 92 to assess the students' essays.

Extra research task

Ask students to research another country's education system by interviewing another student or friend. They should take notes and prepare to explain the system to a small group next lesson. They should mention the following:

- the country the education system is used in
- the ages that students start and finish school
- the size of the classes
- the hours (how long is each class; when does school start and finish)
- the subjects that are taught
- whether the classes are teacher- or student-focused
- their opinions of the advantages and disadvantages of the system.

Allow students planning and practice time before explaining the system to their group. To keep students listening, ask them to write at least two questions to ask at the end. Afterwards, ask the class which education systems they found interesting and why.

CRITICAL THINKING SKILLS Argument: Persuasion through reasons

This page requires students to think more deeply about written arguments from a critical thinking perspective—the reasons why an author might use persuasive techniques and how the audience might affect the way arguments are presented.

Cultural awareness

Some education systems focus less on analysis or author agenda than in Western educational contexts. At advanced levels, an awareness and understanding of the more subtle messages underlying a text is greatly beneficial for both receptive and productive skills, but these may not come easily. The best way to help your students is to consistently develop their critical thinking skills by drawing attention to the author, audience, context, and purpose of a text. Ask questions in classes such as *Who wrote this text? What do you think his/her opinion is? Is he/she for or against the topic? Why? Is the author trying to persuade the audience? How? Which words and phrases does he/she use to do this? Are the arguments relevant/clear/logical/persuasive?*

If possible, read this *Critical thinking skills* page in class. Read through it with the students and encourage them to discuss the following:

- whether they already notice an author's intentions and consider their own audience when writing
- what the benefit of doing this might be for them personally
- how they think they could start to take some of the advice immediately and work it into their regular study practices
- how they think they could use some of the techniques in class
- how these skills might help them if they were studying at university in an English speaking country. Tell students that you will ask them to report whether they have noticed or used any persuasion techniques by the end of next week.

UNIT 8 CHANGE

Reading	Identifying concepts and theories
Critical thinking	Inferring criticism
Language development	Idiomatic language Participle clauses
Writing	Report writing

Ask students to look at the picture and say what they think it shows. Ask questions to stimulate ideas: *Where are the men? What are they doing? How do you think the picture relates to the unit title, Change?*

Background information

The picture shows workers in a car factory, encapsulating the essence of a Ford production line. American Henry Ford started his own car factory assembly line in the early 1900s. This was one of the first production lines where each worker would specialize in making or connecting just one or two parts of a whole item. Workers found factory conditions challenging because of the repetitive nature of their work. High numbers of workers left the company, so Ford introduced incentives such as higher wages and the chance to buy the cars that they manufactured. Many elements of Henry Ford's business practices remain in factory production today.

Discussion point

As a lead-in, ask the class how they think the factory in this picture differs from modern factories. Elicit differences in the equipment (most work seems to be being done by hand—few machines are visible); the clothing (no specific uniform / overalls); health and safety (no standard protective goggles or reinforced footwear); the workers (all men, one very young boy in the background). Record any useful vocabulary on the board.

Ask students to discuss the questions in pairs or groups of three. Monitor their discussions, encouraging them to expand their answers by giving reasons and examples of specific companies or products. Afterwards, ask the groups to share some of their ideas. As a follow-up, ask the class if they can give examples of any other machines or technology that has changed very rapidly during their lifetime.

Vocabulary preview

1 Ask students to work in pairs. Point out that some of the words in the sentences may be new, but they should discuss all the sentences without checking the meanings as they will have the chance to research any new words later. When going over the answers, ask students to read the full definitions with the words in context and then say whether they are true or false. Assist with pronunciation of new words where necessary. Point out that *incentivize* is a good example of the use of suffixes for word building as covered in Unit 6 (*incentive* being the root word and the suffix *-ize* forming the verb).

ANSWERS

1 F 2 T 3 F 4 F 5 T 6 T 7 F 8 F

2 Students work together to correct the false sentences. Again, ask them to say full sentences when giving answers.

POSSIBLE ANSWERS

1 A *business model* is an outline of a good business structure.
3 If you *drive a company forward*, you lead the company with a view for progression and success.
4 If you *empower* someone, you give that person a sense of power.
7 A *mentoring scheme* involves experienced people supporting and advising less experienced people.
8 If you *execute* a strategy, you carry it out.

READING Leadership and change management

Word count 1,121

Background information

With the rapid modernization and increasing competitiveness of the global economy in the past few decades, companies and organizations are constantly changing. Change management has become a whole industry in itself with many companies dedicated to consulting on, researching, and implementing change in the workplace. Research into change management extends through many scientific disciplines including physics, sociology, and psychology.

Before you read

As a lead-in, write the title, *Leadership and change management,* on the board and ask students what they think it means. Write some of their ideas on the board and then put them into pairs to discuss the questions. Point out that it may help them to write brief notes and perhaps organize them in a word web or a table as you will ask them to share ideas with the class afterwards. Record any useful vocabulary on the board.

Global reading

Before referring students to the *Identifying concepts and theories* box, ask them if they know the meaning of *concept* and *theory*. Ask them if they can explain how these are different from an argument. Refer them to the *Identifying concepts and theories* box and ask them to read it to check whether they were correct. Emphasize the final two sentences in the box which explain that in academic texts authors often present concepts or theories, but these don't necessarily reflect their own ideas. In some situations, they will be expected to evaluate concepts or theories and then write or present their own arguments or conclusions in relation to them.

1 Read through the instructions with the class. Elicit or explain the meaning of *excerpt* (a section of text from a longer article). Encourage students to underline the key words in the descriptions before completing the exercise. Students do the exercise individually and then compare answers in pairs.

ANSWERS

a Kotter's eight-step approach to change management
b Fisher's model of personal change
c Lewin's Unfreeze, Change, Refreeze model

Exam tip

The skills practiced in exercises 1 to 3 are useful for completing tasks in the Academic IELTS Reading Test. Exercises 1 and 3 practice matching tasks. Remind students that they should take time to skim-read a text before starting on the questions (even if they feel under pressure because of time constraints). Skimming and scanning help them to navigate a text better, and with more confidence. This can lead to greater accuracy and faster completion of the tasks.

Exercise 2 practices skills required for completing *True, False, Not Given* tasks. Remind students that underlining the key words (in conjunction with skimming and scanning) can help them to find the answers more quickly.

2 If your students are studying for the IELTS Test or equivalent, review the content of the *Exam tip* box and remind them of any key exam strategies (in this case, underlining key words in the questions). Check that students understand the meaning of *influential*. Set a time limit of 2–2½ minutes for them to complete the exercise. Watch to see whether they are using the skills and strategies that have been introduced in the book so far—it may be necessary to review some of these for consolidation. Allow them to compare answers before checking as a class.

ANSWERS

1 F, they should keep innovating
2 T
3 F, 70% fail
4 F, their journeys are different

3 Remind students to annotate the texts (writing the number of the question that is answered beside the correct part of the text, and in this case they should include the initials *L*, *K*, or *F* that represent each model) as they complete an exercise or exam task. This way if they disagree on any answers or have made errors, they can locate them quickly in the text. Ask students to compare answers in pairs or small groups before checking them as a class.

ANSWERS

1 L, K
2 L, K
3 L
4 F
5 L, K
6 F
7 K
8 L, K, F

4 Draw a large diagram (as shown below) on the board. Students are likely to have seen these before, but they may not have understood them or used them themselves in their own education systems. Ask students: *Do you know what this kind of diagram is called?* (a Venn diagram); *What are they used for?* (showing shared features of a group of things or concepts); *Have you ever used one?*

Background information

Venn diagrams have been used by scientists and mathematicians since the mid-twentieth century to show relations and shared qualities between sets. They are named after the English philosopher and logician John Venn (1834–1923), and became popular in 1880 after he wrote a paper, *On the Diagrammatic and Mechanical Representation of Propositions and Reasonings*, about their use. Similar two-circle diagrams were used by Greek scientist and philosopher Aristotle (384–322 BCE).

ANSWERS

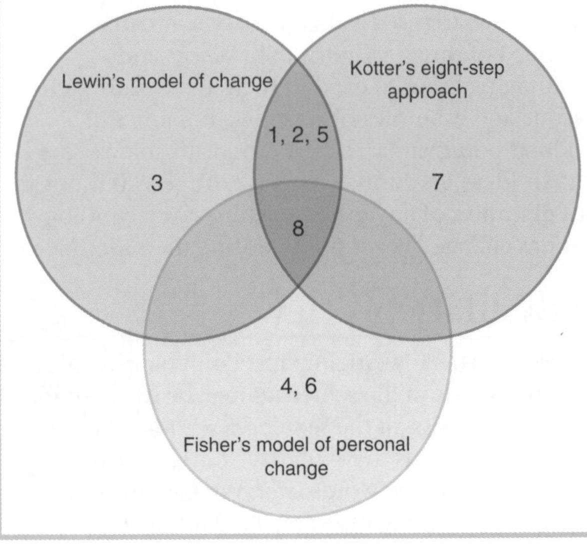

5 Read the question and look at the example with the students. Elicit or explain the meaning of *analogy* (a comparison between two situations or processes that is intended to show that the two are similar). Ask if analogies are commonly used in their languages and elicit some examples. Students complete the exercise on their own and then compare answers in pairs.

ANSWERS

1 Admiring the view too long on a mountain without realizing there is more to climb.
2 An uphill struggle.
3 Melting a block of ice in one shape and refreezing it in another shape.
4 Crossing from one peak to another.

Draw students' attention to the *Academic keywords* box. Ask students if they know the meaning of the words and teach if necessary. Review their pronunciation and stress, and tell students to add them to their vocabulary notebooks. If following the class wiki project, this unit's wiki group should also add these keywords to the wiki.

EXTENSION ACTIVITY

Suggest that students make a Venn diagram of their own. Ask them to choose a topic based on an interest or their specialist academic subject. If they have access to the Internet, suggest that they type *make a Venn diagram* into a search engine. There are many websites which offer this facility. If they don't have Internet access, they could draw their own diagram. Ask them to prepare a very brief presentation (approximately one to one and a half minutes) to give to a partner, group, or the class to explain their diagram in the next lesson.

Critical thinking skill

Cultural awareness

It can be very challenging for students to understand the underlying, or inferred, meanings in a text. This is especially true of students from educational backgrounds where criticizing a published author is not considered appropriate, or from countries where the language is more direct and meanings are less likely to be hidden. A good way to support students with this is to help them to consider the author's agenda when reading. Ask concept questions during lessons and when checking answers, for example, *What do you think the author's stance is—does he/she think it's a good idea/theory/practice? Why or why not? How do you know? Which words does the writer use to infer criticism?*

SUPPORTING CRITICAL THINKING

The questions in this section require students to consider the author's views in detail, analyzing the language she uses to infer criticism. Some students may find this challenging (see the *Cultural awareness* box) so allow plenty of time for pair and group discussion. Again, encourage students to annotate their texts and notice the language that the author uses. Suggest that they try these activities with other academic texts or newspaper articles. They could do this with a study partner if it helps. Remind them that this type of textual analysis (looking at author intention, opinion, and agenda) can lead to a much greater understanding of academic texts so they should include it as part of their regular independent study.

As a lead-in, write *inferring criticism* on the board. Ask students if they know what *infer* means (suggest something without directly saying it). Ask students if it is common for authors to infer criticism in their language. Refer them to the *Inferring criticism* box and give them time to read it. Afterwards, ask them the meanings of the underlined words in the example. Explain that adverbs with negative meanings, for example, *unnecessarily, mistakenly, obviously* are often used when criticizing. Here the adverb *yet* means *still* and is often used in formal or academic English.

1 Ask students to do the task on their own and then discuss answers in pairs. Elicit or point out the use of the adverb *mistakenly*, and the phrases *far too long* (*far* meaning *much*) and *not appreciating* (meaning *not realizing*) to infer criticism.

ANSWERS

... while other companies have mistakenly spent far too long looking at the scenery, not appreciating that further heights were there to be scaled.

2 Ask students to do the exercise and then compare answers with a partner. Emphasize the importance of giving reasons for their choices. Tell them to discuss which words helped them to decide. Check answers as a class.

ANSWERS

The writer is critical of:

2 while other companies have mistakenly spent far too long looking at the scenery, not appreciating that further heights were there to be scaled.
4 It is the final stage which companies may struggle to apply in today's fast-moving world ...
5 Yet one of the biggest reasons ... / It is easy for a change management strategy to focus solely on systems, but ...

The writer is not critical of:

1 Successful companies such as Apple®, Google, and Amazon are all examples of industry leaders which

understand that they still have a mountain to climb, while …

6 … provides businesses with a comprehensive and solid understanding of how much of an impact change may have on employees across the board.

The writer is both critical and not critical of 3:
… planning and executing a change strategy can be an uphill struggle (not critical) with organisations often pulling the plug on strategies at the first sign of difficulty. (critical)

Developing critical thinking

Put students into pairs or small groups for the discussion task. Listen to their discussions and take note of any useful vocabulary or points to expand at the feedback stage. Remember to mention any well thought-out ideas and critical thinking techniques that you heard students using to help them gain confidence and provide extra incentive to try out new skills next time.

SUPPORTING CRITICAL THINKING

The questions in this section require the students to evaluate the change models outlined in the text from a range of perspectives. To maximize the chances to exercise critical thinking, take a step-by-step approach for question 1. First, ask students to take brief notes of the key features of each model. Then ask them to brainstorm the challenges that are faced when a large company goes through major change. Finally, they should discuss which model would best suit a large company, giving reasons and examples for their choices.

EXTENSION ACTIVITY

Put students into pairs or groups of three and draw their attention to the illustration of the man on the tightrope in the text. Ask them to read the words that are suspended from the rope (*anxiety, happiness, fear, threat, guilt, depression, gradual acceptance, moving forward*). Tell them to discuss the meanings and decide whether they would apply to management, staff, or both, and why. Ask them to add more words to the list, again explaining why those affected would feel that way.

For stronger classes, expand this exercise by getting students to work in their groups to devise their own leadership and change management model. Tell them that they should be prepared to explain their model clearly and concisely to the class (approximately one to one and a half minutes). You could allow more time for this task and get them to prepare visuals to accompany longer, more formal presentations (approximately five minutes).

Language development: Idiomatic language

Cultural awareness

In some cultures, it is acceptable to use idiomatic expressions in academic writing. You may find that students use expressions in opinion essays to show that people have differing views. If your students overuse certain expressions in their writing or speech, it may be that they are translations of common expressions in their language. In this case, it would be worth setting aside some extra class time to discuss idioms; valuing them, but also emphasizing that they are not considered appropriate in English in an academic context. Generally, students can find idioms frustrating as it is often difficult to work out the meanings from context. Point out that despite this, it is always worth trying before reaching for a dictionary. Another good way to find out the meanings is to ask a native speaker.

As a lead-in, ask the class: *What is an idiom? Do you know any English idioms? Are idioms common in your language?* Elicit some examples if possible and write them on the board. Emphasize that although idiomatic language is not considered appropriate for academic texts, it is common in English, and knowing some will improve their general knowledge and understanding.

1 Allow students to do exercise 1 individually or in pairs if they wish. When going over the answers, ask them to give the full definition of the idioms, for example, *"Mountain to climb" means a difficult task to reach a goal.* Encourage them to make a note of the idioms in their vocabulary notebooks.

ANSWERS
1 b 2 d 3 e 4 a 5 c

2 Give students time to read the text and consider the meaning of the idioms, then put them into pairs or small groups to discuss their ideas. Point out that this is another good opportunity to practice giving definitions, saying, for example, *I think "beg to differ" means …*

This is a good place to use the video resource *Shock to the system*. It is located in the Video resources section of the digital component. Alternatively, remind students about the video so they can do this at home. If following the class wiki project, this unit's wiki group can add some of the words from this section to the class wiki.

3 Draw students' attention to the definitions and ask them to do the exercise individually before comparing answers with a partner.

ANSWERS

1 politely	6 changes
2 not knowing	7 supporting
3 most	8 fail
4 definitely	9 more
5 basic	10 easy

Language development: Participle clauses

Students will have read participle clauses whilst studying, but they are unlikely to be using them regularly and with confidence at this stage. Emphasize that they are common in academic writing and that using them themselves will improve their academic style. For consolidation, try to review this structure regularly in subsequent lessons and praise students when they use it correctly when writing or in presentations. Give students plenty of time to study the examples in the *Participle clauses* box and ask you questions before moving on to exercise 1.

1 As this exercise is likely to present a challenge, give students plenty of time to rewrite the sentences and allow them to discuss ideas as they work. Check answers as a class, writing the correct sentences on the board if necessary.

ANSWERS

1 Wanting to create a change strategy, senior managers brought in a consultant.
2 While reading the consultant's report, they realized they needed to organize a meeting.
3 Attended by all management, the meeting took place in the boardroom.
4 On hearing about the report, the managers had a lot of questions.

2 Again, allow plenty of writing and discussion time. Monitor and help where necessary. If students are confident, allow them to write the answers on the board and correct where necessary.

ANSWERS

1 While/On hearing about the changes, some staff members became angry.
2 Some staff members resigned, wanting things to stay the same. / Wanting things to stay the same, some staff members resigned.
3 After explaining the situation, / Having explained the situation, managers received positive feedback from the staff.
4 Having received training, all staff successfully coped with the changes. / All staff, after receiving training, successfully coped with the changes.

3 Students complete the sentences individually and then discuss their answers in pairs. Ask confident students for example sentences. Write any good examples on the board and suggest that the students copy them.

EXTENSION ACTIVITY

Ask students to find two or three pictures of people in a newspaper or magazine and write caption sentences describing the scene. Explain that they should write one sentence using a participle clause for each sentence. Suggest that they refer back to exercises 1 to 3 of this section for ideas. This activity could be done in class (if you prepare by taking in some old newspapers and magazines) or for homework as a review activity.

WRITING Report writing

As a lead-in, ask students to think of situations where a report might be required, e.g., school or work (a person or team's performance); business; statistics; the results of a study or discovery; an inquiry into a crime, disaster, or accident. Elicit their ideas, and write any useful words and phrases on the board. Read through the instructions with the students and ask: *What features should a good report include?*

Writing skill

Ask students to read the *Report writing* box and check whether the features they mentioned in the lead-in activity are included. Ask them to briefly recap the key features of a report.

1 Ask students to skim-read the report and briefly tell you the gist of it before starting on exercise 1. Ask them do the exercise individually, but allow them to discuss ideas with a partner if they find it helps. Give them time to compare answers and explain that you will check them after exercise 2.

2 Remind students that bullet points are often used in reports to present key points simply and concisely. Write a colon (:) on the board, and ask students if they know what it is called and how it is used. Elicit or explain that they are often used in reports before a list of items or examples. These may be divided by commas, numbers, letters, or bullet points. For example:

Ingredients: flour, sugar, eggs, and milk

Factory rules:

1) all visitors must report to main reception

2) safety helmets must be worn at all times

3) mobile phones must be switched off

Put students into pairs or groups of three for this exercise. Allow them plenty of time to read the report and decide how it should best be structured. Monitor and assist when needed. Take note of any important points about structure and punctuation to feed back on afterwards.

POSSIBLE ANSWER
Buckson's supermarket

Introduction
Buckson's is a local grocery store located in a large residential area of the town. It first opened in 1924 and has been a family business ever since. Because sales have been dropping slowly for the last ten years, research has been conducted to find out the reasons why.

Research method
The research involved:
- Face-to-face interviews with 30 Buckson's customers.
- Face-to-face interviews with 30 customers of Buckson's closest rival supermarket, Shop Mart.

The interviews lasted approximately ten minutes and included 15 questions.

Results
The results of the research established that:
- Customers are purchasing fewer items due to long lines at the check-out, no Internet presence, and no delivery service.
- Customers believe Buckson's goods to be of high quality (e.g., bakery goods are freshly made). Several customers said, "They make the best cakes in town."
- Customers think the staff are friendlier and more helpful than at the nearest competitor.

Conclusions
Overall analysis of the results suggests that customers would be happy to pay Buckson's prices if they were able to receive a faster check-out service and the opportunity to order food online or in the store which is later delivered.

Recommendations
It is highly recommended that Buckson's:
- Invest in a higher speed Internet connection and faster scanners to avoid long lines at the check-out.
- Create an online shopping facility, including a shopping app that can be downloaded onto mobile phones.
- Purchase vans in which food can be delivered.
- Ensure that current staff members are able to adapt to the new changes and continue to provide a high-quality service to customers.

WRITING TASK

Refer students to the box at the top of the page which outlines the audience, context, and purpose. Ask them to read the report and then discuss the purpose in pairs.

POSSIBLE ANSWER
The purpose of the report is to make recommendations as to what the modernization program should involve.

Read the instructions and make sure that students know what they are expected to do. Emphasize that they are only required to finish the report—they don't need to write a new introduction.

Brainstorm, plan, and write

Put students into pairs and ask them to discuss the questions. Remind them of how the critical thinking exercises earlier in the unit considered change from a range of perspectives. Encourage them to do this when evaluating the effectiveness of their suggestions.

Remind students of the importance of planning before writing. This is particularly obvious when writing a report which must be logical and concise. Ask them to work individually to write their headings and decide on the structure. Give them a time limit of ten minutes to do this, and then ask them to discuss and evaluate their plans in pairs. At this stage, monitor and advise where necessary. Make sure that students are happy with their plans before moving on to the writing stage.

Each report will be different, but suggest the following headings: Introduction, Problems, Possible Solutions, Recommendations, Conclusions. Under Recommendations, there can be subheadings to deal with each suggestion. Suggestions could include:

- Raise awareness of the need for change through meetings.
- Train staff to manage the changes effectively.
- Consult staff at all times, getting their ideas and opinions.
- Set up a mentor scheme or 1:1 counseling to discuss the progress of the changes.
- Have team-building tasks to keep everyone looking toward the same goal.
- Incentivize staff so they feel motivated.
- Hold regular meetings to report progress and give staff positive feedback.

Do the writing task in class so that you can monitor and assist students where necessary. Tell them that they should write approximately 300 words, and remind them of the audience and context of their report. Set a time limit of approximately 40–60 minutes for the first draft. Monitor and assist students where necessary.

Share, rewrite, and edit

Ask students to exchange their reports with a partner. Encourage them to use the Peer review checklist on page 109 when they are evaluating their partner's report. Give students around ten minutes for this stage. Remind them to use the checklist to make constructive comments. Tell them to number the parts of the report that they want to comment on and then take notes on a separate piece of paper to share with their partner as they give feedback. The student whose work is being analyzed should respond by accepting, rejecting, or asking for further explanation and clarification. They can then write their own comments on their report to help them when they rewrite.

Ask students to rewrite and edit their reports for homework. Encourage them to take into consideration their partner's feedback when rewriting. Remind them that they should write a plan even for rewrites. You could even insist that they hand in a plan with every writing assignment for marking. This way you can see how well they are organizing their ideas before writing. Use the photocopiable *Unit assignment checklist* on page 93 to assess the students' reports.

Extra research task

Ask students to research and prepare a short presentation of approximately one to one and a half minutes outlining a change management model that interests them, and giving the advantages and disadvantages of it. Explain that this need not be related to changes to organizations; it could be to people generally, i.e., accepting personal change, or to technological change (as in Roger's Technology Adoption Curve). They should provide at least one diagram or visual to illustrate their model. If they have access to the Internet, they could type *change management model* into a search engine to find ideas. Some examples of other change management models are:

- the McKinsey 7-S Model
- ADKAR
- Bridge's Transition Model
- Roger's Technology Adoption Curve.

On the day of the presentations, allow students time to review and practice. Ask the audience to take notes so that they could summarize the main points afterwards.

STUDY SKILLS Editing your work

Cultural awareness

Many students will be from educational backgrounds where only the teacher marks their work. However, in English speaking universities they will need to become comfortable with both self and peer evaluation. This may be a difficult concept for students from cultures where admitting errors can result in loss of face—a great sense of shame and humiliation. It's a good idea to discuss such issues openly and explain how these skills will help them to produce higher quality work. Try to help build your students' confidence in doing this gradually throughout their course of study.

Getting started

Refer students to the title *Editing your work*, and ask them whether they are expected to do this in their native education system. Put them into pairs to discuss the questions. When they have finished, ask them to feed back the answers they discussed and write any useful vocabulary on the board.

Scenario

Refer students to the picture of Faisal. Ask them to skim-read the scenario and then briefly tell you the gist. Tell them to read the scenario again and follow the instructions. Give them some time to think about the answer and take notes before putting them into pairs to discuss it. In the feedback session, write some of their ideas on the board.

POSSIBLE ANSWER

Faisal left time between writing his report and revising it. He checked that the information all led to his conclusions. However, he did not check that the report was structured in a way that readers could follow, he did not proofread it, and he did not leave enough time to revise the report effectively.

EXTENSION ACTIVITY

If you have done the rewrite of the report in class, ask students to take it home and try some of the strategies mentioned on the *Study skills* page. Suggest that they take notes, and be prepared to discuss what type of changes they made and how well the strategies worked for them. If they haven't done the rewrite in class, set this task for the end of the next lesson as consolidation.

Consider it

Ask students to work in pairs or groups of three to discuss the strategies. Monitor and assist with prompts where necessary.

Over to you

Ask students to stay in their pairs or groups, read the instructions, and then discuss the questions. Afterwards, ask for volunteers to share their answers. If students are reluctant to admit their mistakes (see the *Cultural awareness* box), write some common errors on the board and ask the students how they could try to prevent repeating these in future.

UNIT 9 FLOW

Reading	Identifying links
Critical thinking	Identifying logical fallacies
Language development	Verbs and expressions with prepositions
	Expressing causality
Writing	Writing effective conclusions

Ask students to look at the picture and say what they think it shows. Ask questions to stimulate ideas: *Which country do you think this is? Why? From the picture and the title, Flow, what do you think the topic of this unit will be?*

Background information

The picture shows a man in Guilin, China practicing the ancient tradition of cormorant fishing. The birds are trained to dive from the bamboo raft into the water to catch fish and then return them to the fishermen. The fishing usually takes place at dusk, and the boats are illuminated by lamplight. This tradition has existed on rivers and lakes in China for hundreds of years. In the past, it was a thriving industry, but modern, commercial, fishing methods have taken over, and nowadays the tradition in many areas is maintained by the tourism industry.

Discussion point

As a warmer, put students into pairs and give them a time limit of one minute to write the names of as many of the world's major rivers as possible. Tell them not to worry about spelling. Afterwards, ask them to count up how many names they have and then to compare lists with another pair to see if they have any different rivers. While they are comparing lists, write on the board: *Which country is the river in? Are there any major cities along it? How do people use the river?* Ask confident students to choose one or two of the rivers they discussed to feed back on. Record any useful vocabulary on the board.

Ask students to discuss the questions in pairs or groups of three. Check that they understand the meaning of *threaten* and *harm*. Suggest that for question 3, they could make a mind map with these headwords: *the economy, transportation, floods, energy,* and *tourism*. Monitor their discussions, encouraging them to expand their answers by giving reasons and examples. Ask students to share some of their ideas afterwards and record any useful vocabulary on the board.

Vocabulary preview

1 Ask students to skim-read the text for the gist and then draw their attention to the words in the box. If there is new vocabulary, allow them time to discuss it in pairs before checking the meanings and pronunciation. Ask students to complete the text on their own. Tell them that you will check the answers after they have completed exercise 2.

2 Ask students to compare answers. Afterwards, check answers as a class with students reading the words in context. Then ask them to work together to write the definitions. Ask confident pairs to give example definitions.

ANSWERS

1 civilizations
2 soil
3 crops
4 Irrigation
5 commodities
6 domesticate
7 Trade
8 flourish

READING How rivers made civilisation

Word count 1,242

Background information

The word *Mesopotamia*, meaning "between the rivers," was used by the Greeks to describe the area of land between the Euphrates and Tigris rivers over 6,000 years ago. This area, which now includes modern Iraq and Syria, is often referred to as the cradle of civilization. It is thought that the geography and rich natural resources in Mesopotamia led to a number of important discoveries and inventions which over thousands of years helped to shape modern civilization. The Mesopotamians invented the wheel and developed important agricultural practices such as animal domestication and herding. They also developed early writing in the form of pictograms (pictures that represented a word), and built the world's first cities and monuments.

Before you read

Draw students' attention to the title of the reading, *How rivers made civilisation*, and ask them what they think the text will be about. Write some of their ideas on the board and then check whether they know anything about Mesopotamia (see the *Background information* box above). Put students into pairs to discuss the statements and then check the answers. (Note: the answers are upside down just below the exercise. Do not allow students to read the text at this stage.)

Global reading

Before referring students to the *Identifying links* box, ask them what they think identifying links in a text means. Refer them to the *Identifying links* box and ask them to read it to check whether they were correct. Emphasize that identifying links between texts, the real world, and their own general knowledge and experience is an extremely important part of independent study and requires good critical thinking skills.

Read through the instructions with the class. Put students into pairs or groups of three and ask them to discuss possible answers without looking at the text. Give them around five minutes for this and then ask them to feed back. Write some of their ideas on the board. Set a time limit of approximately one and a half minutes for students to skim-read the text and discuss the gist. Ask them to complete the exercise individually, but allow them to discuss answers if it helps. Encourage them to use important exam techniques such as underlining the key words in the sentences and annotating the text. Check answers as a class.

ANSWERS

1. All of these cultures arose from rivers.
2. The rivers flooded in these places, leaving behind fertile soil that was excellent for growing crops.
3. Disputes over water created a need for writing so that clear ownership records could be kept.
4. Some observers say that the sorrow and mourning found in ancient Mesopotamian literature can still be found in modern Iraqi culture today.
5. The Nile gave ancient Egyptians valuable commodities for trade while also serving as the trade route itself.
6. Because it was virtually impossible for an invading army to cross the desert, ancient Egypt enjoyed a stable government that was mostly free of war and conflict.

Draw students' attention to the *Academic keywords* box. Ask them if they know the meaning of the words and teach them if necessary. Review their pronunciation and stress, and ask students to add them to their vocabulary notebooks. If following the class wiki project, this unit's wiki group should also add these keywords to the wiki.

EXTENSION ACTIVITY

Ask students to think of their hometown, and brainstorm key information about its geography, agriculture, trade, and economy. Tell them that they should also consider whether these contribute to its location. Give them a time limit of approximately five minutes to takes notes. Explain that you will ask them to share their ideas with other students afterwards. After the time limit, put students into pairs or small groups to discuss their hometowns. While they are doing this, write on the board: *How are new towns and cities formed in the twenty-first century? What is their location related to? What are the problems associated with them? Are new cities or parts of cities appearing? Are historical or older cities expanding rapidly? Are industries changing?*

Allow plenty of time for the discussion. Monitor and take note of interesting points to expand and relevant topic-related vocabulary. Praise students who extend the conversation with reasons, examples, or follow-up questions.

Critical thinking skill

Cultural awareness

Students whose native language doesn't use modal verbs, or uses them in a different way, may struggle to identify and understand examples of logical fallacy. Such statements often contain speculative modals such as *must, might, may,* and *could*. If this applies to your class, make an extra effort to support your students with modals and their usage. Study how they are used in academic texts and make a point of checking that students understand the underlying meaning of sentences containing them. Ask questions such as, *Is this a logical/valid argument? Why or why not? How do you know? Which words suggest that to you?*

SUPPORTING CRITICAL THINKING

The questions in this section require students to analyze arguments from the text and say why they are logical fallacies. If you think that your students will find this challenging (see the *Cultural awareness* box above) allow plenty of time for pair and group discussion. Monitor and take note of any useful points to raise with the class during feedback. Again, encourage students to notice the language that the author uses (in this case speculative phrases containing modals such as *must be, must have been, must cause*, adverbs *probably, likely*, and the verb *assume*). Remind them that they can practice these skills with other academic texts or newspaper articles either alone or with a study partner.

As a lead-in, write *Identifying logical fallacies* on the board. Ask students if they know what a *fallacy* is. If they don't, teach it or allow them to look it up in their monolingual dictionaries (an idea or belief that is false but that many people think is true [source: Macmillan Dictionary Online]). Refer them to the *Identifying logical fallacies* box, and give them time to read it and ask you any necessary questions.

1 Put students into pairs to do the exercise. There are no absolute answers for this question. Monitor and assist where necessary, encouraging students to explain their ideas in detail. Allow pairs time to compare answers before asking for some example reasons for each sentence to list on the board.

2 Suggest that students do the exercise individually and then compare answers with a partner. Encourage them to give reasons for their answers.

ANSWERS
1 c 2 a 3 b

3 Students stay in their pairs to discuss the question. Point out that *the kind of logical fallacy* relates to the three types mentioned in the *Identifying logical fallacies* box. Ask them to also say which words show that these are logical fallacies.

ANSWERS
1 confusing correlation and causation
2 after, therefore, because
3 argument from ignorance

Developing critical thinking

SUPPORTING CRITICAL THINKING

The questions in this section require students to draw on their own opinions and experience as well as the information in the text. To extend the exercise, and maximize opportunity for critical thinking and negotiation, organize a "pyramid" discussion. Put students into pairs to brainstorm their lists and think of at least two reasons why the inventions are vital to civilization. Ask them to choose the five most important and rank them. Explain that their reasons must be clear and logical because they will have to try to convince their classmates that their choices are right. Get pairs to join together to make groups of four, compare lists, and rank again. Continue the process, doubling the group size, until the whole class can reach a consensus on the most important invention or discovery.

Students discuss the questions in pairs or small groups, or have a pyramid discussion as mentioned in the *Supporting critical thinking* box above. Monitor unobtrusively, making sure that no student dominates the conversation and taking note of any useful vocabulary or points to expand at the feedback stage. Remember to mention any well thought-out ideas and critical thinking techniques that you heard students using to help them gain confidence and provide extra incentive to try out new skills next time.

EXTENSION ACTIVITY

Put students into pairs or groups of three and ask them to choose the invention or development that they think is the most important for civilization. Tell them to prepare a short presentation (approximately two minutes) to the class explaining:

- what the invention/development is
- why it is the most important for civilization.

At the end, the class can vote for the most convincing presentation.

Language development: Verbs and expressions with prepositions

Cultural awareness

Prepositions can cause great frustration for some students especially as there are no clear rules. Some languages do not use prepositions at all, and many use prepositions more, less, or in a different way. Whatever the native language of your students, it is inevitable that they will make mistakes such as omitting, overusing, or misusing them. Explain that they may find that learning prepositions is easier if they view them lexically (as vocabulary) rather than grammatically. By this stage in the course, the students will already be familiar with collocations. Prepositions can be noticed and recorded in a similar way. A good way to help your students notice how prepositions are used is to give them an academic text, and get them to circle all the prepositions and the words and expressions that go with them. Point out that they can do this during independent study, too.

As a lead-in, ask the class: *What is a preposition? Do you have them in your language? Are they used in the same way? Do you ever have problems with prepositions?* Elicit some answers and examples, and write them on the board. Explain that verb expressions with prepositions are common in academic texts and learning some as whole phrases will be very useful to them. Give students time to read the information in the *Verbs and expressions with prepositions* box and ask any necessary questions.

1 Ask students to complete the sentences individually and then compare answers. When checking the answers, get them to read the full sentences with expressions in context. Encourage them to make a note of the verb expressions with prepositions in their vocabulary notebooks and add them to the class wiki if relevant.

ANSWERS

1 had an effect on	6 resulted in
2 arose from	7 lead to
3 known as	8 resulted from
4 made for	9 gave rise to
5 made use of	

2 You might find it useful to do this exercise in two stages to ensure students get the full benefit without rushing on to check the text. Ask students to complete the sentences individually and then compare answers before moving on to check their answers against the text.

ANSWERS
1 with **2** of **3** at **4** of **5** to **6** to

This is a good place to use the video resource *Volcanic flow*. It is located in the Video resources section of the digital component. Alternatively, remind students about the video so they can do this at home. If you are following the class wiki project, this unit's wiki group can add some of the words from this section to the class wiki.

EXTENSION ACTIVITY

Bring several different academic texts (of the same length and level of challenge) to the class. Divide students into pairs or small groups and give each group a text.

Give them an adequate time limit (approximately 15 minutes), and ask them to circle all the verb expressions with prepositions and then record them in their notebooks. They should write the meanings and two example sentences for each expression. Afterwards, get students to teach some of their expressions to the class and invite further examples to write on the board. If your class is confident, allow them to "take over" the classroom and write on the board themselves, asking you for input where necessary.

Language development: Expressing causality

Your students are likely to have studied causality before, but this section gives a useful overview of a range of phrases and adverbs which express this. Emphasize that it is an important academic skill to be able to show that you are aware of the causes and consequences of events. Give students plenty of time to study the examples in the *Expressing causality* box and ask questions if necessary. To consolidate, put students into pairs and ask them to re-read each example sentence and write another example sentence. Afterwards, ask for some examples to write on the board.

1 This exercise may present a challenge especially as some sentences require the clauses to swap positions. Give students plenty of time to write the sentences and allow them to discuss ideas with a partner as they write. Check answers as a class, writing the correct sentences on the board if necessary.

ANSWERS

1 The Nile's yearly floods gave rise to excellent farmland.
2 The development of money resulted in more efficient trade.
3 As Egypt was the strongest culture in the region, it dominated trade.
4 The gentle nature of the Nile's floods had an effect on the ancient Egyptians' outlook on life.
5 Water was scarce; consequently, conflict was common in Mesopotamia.
6 Political instability in Mesopotamia resulted from a lack of natural barriers to invasion.
7 Disputes over land were a factor in the development of writing and laws.
8 The impact of rivers on the rise of civilization is hard to overstate.

2 This exercise gives a valuable opportunity for students to use the target language in an authentic way, so allow plenty of writing and discussion time. Monitor and help where necessary.

3 Students compare answers and peer correct, rewriting their sentences as necessary. Afterwards, ask confident students for some examples. For further practice, write some incorrect sentences on the board and invite the students to correct them. These should be based on, but not identical to, a student error to avoid loss of face / embarrassment.

WRITING A cause and effect essay

Background information

The ability to understand and express cause and effect relationships is essential to academic success. If your students are struggling with identifying or distinguishing between causes and effects, or having difficulty seeing the relationships between them, it may be useful to present them in lists or as word webs with the cause as the headword, e.g.,

Cause	Effect
the Nile provided food, wealth, and security	the Nile flourished
warfare was common	Mesopotamia was vulnerable to invasion
difficult circumstances	a pessimistic outlook on life

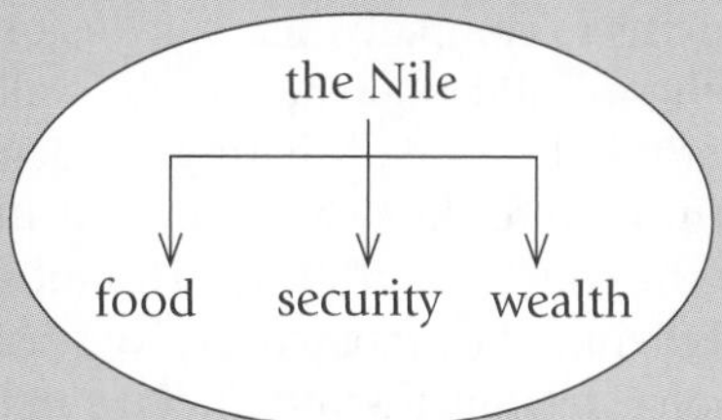

As a lead-in, ask students to think of situations where they may need to express causality (e.g., when reporting the results of an experiment; to explain causes or effects of something; to explain why an event happened). Elicit their ideas, and write any useful words and phrases on the board.

Writing skill

Ask students to read the *Writing effective conclusions* box and ask any necessary questions. Ask concept questions such as: *What should you include in a concluding paragraph?* (restate the main idea and the key supporting points); *What should you do to consider your reader*? (make sure the topic is relevant to the modern reader's concerns); *How should you extend the main idea?* (by discussing its implications). Remind students to make sure the conclusion gives a clear and unambiguous answer to the question and makes it clear to the reader that the essay is finished.

1 Ask students to skim-read the conclusion and briefly recall the gist before allowing them to move on to exercise 1. Ask them to do the exercise individually and then compare answers.

ANSWER
The writer followed tips 1 and 2.

2 Put students into pairs and ask them to decide on a writer. Emphasize that this is a joint piece of writing so they should work together to produce it. Explain that discussing the wording, and then rephrasing and correcting, is a valuable part of the process, and speaking is therefore as important as writing. Monitor and make sure that students work collaboratively in this way, helping where necessary.

POSSIBLE ANSWER
Almost every part of our daily lives—from traffic laws to text messages to imported fruit and vegetables—has its roots in the early river valley civilisations. By taking advantage of the ideal conditions these rivers created for agriculture, trade, and—in the case of Egypt—unity and stability, these ancient peoples laid the foundations of our societies today: writing, laws, agriculture, calendars, trade, and much more. The history of these civilisations also highlights the importance of the environment to human societies; we still depend on rivers today and ought to treat them with greater care.

3 Ask students to compare their conclusions. If space allows, these could be posted on the walls around the classroom for ease of sharing. Students could then go around reading each one, and afterwards vote for the conclusion they felt was most effective. Remind them to be prepared to give reasons for their choice, relating them to the tips in the *Writing effective conclusions* box if possible.

WRITING TASK

Refer students to the box at the top of the page which outlines the audience, context, and purpose. Draw their attention to the mind map and explain that this is a very clear way to organize their ideas on paper before writing. Ask them to study the mind map and then discuss the links in pairs. If students are finding this challenging, extend the exercise by asking them to choose more information to analyze the links. They could compare ideas with other pairs or in small groups. Ask groups to report back and write the best examples on the board.

POSSIBLE ANSWERS
Agriculture: The violent, unpredictable floods of the Yellow River created excellent farmland.
History and politics: The river allowed people to travel between different communities; this united the different ethnic groups along the river.
Culture: Because they were surrounded by mountains and deserts, they were isolated from the world outside China.
Economics: Because the river was good for agriculture, it made the area the most prosperous region in China.

Brainstorm, plan, and write

Put students into pairs to do the *Brainstorm* exercise. Suggest
that they look back at the *Vocabulary preview* section on page 88 and the text for points to consider, for example, agriculture, trade, economics, and politics. Monitor and help with expanding ideas where necessary.

Remind students of the importance of planning and point out that the topics in the *Plan* section will form the main content of their essay. Give them a time limit of ten minutes and ask them to work individually to write their outline or mind maps. After the time limit, ask them to discuss and evaluate their plans in pairs. At this stage, monitor and advise where necessary. Make sure that students are happy with their plans before moving on to the writing stage.

Plan to do the writing task in class so that you can monitor and assist students as they write. Tell them that they should write approximately 300 words, and remind them of the audience and context of their report. Set a time limit of approximately 40–60 minutes for the first draft. Monitor and assist students where necessary. Encourage students to refer to their plans during the writing process.

Share, rewrite, and edit

Ask students to exchange their essays with a partner. Encourage them to use the Peer review checklist on page 109 when they are evaluating their partner's essay. Give students around ten minutes for this stage. Remind them to use the checklist to make constructive comments based on the bullet points. Remind them to number the parts of the essay that they want to comment on and then take notes on a separate piece of paper to share with their partner as they give feedback. The student whose work is being analyzed should respond by accepting, rejecting, or asking for further explanation and clarification. They can then write their own comments on their report to help them when they rewrite.

Ask students to rewrite and edit their essays. Encourage them to take into consideration their partner's feedback when rewriting. Remind them to look back at the *Writing effective conclusions* box on page 94 for tips if necessary. If they are studying for an academic exam, they could do the rewrite under exam conditions, or you could ask them to set themselves a time limit to adhere to at home. Remind them that they should write a plan even for rewrites, and especially in an exam. To ensure that they do this, ask them to hand in a plan with the essay for marking so that you can see how well they are organizing their ideas before writing. Use the photocopiable *Unit assignment checklist* on page 94 to assess the students' essays.

Extra research task

Ask students to research and prepare to write a cause and effect essay. They can choose their own topic, or one from the list below:

- the downturn in the global economy
- the positive effects of a particular food, drink, or form of exercise on health
- the effects of weather pattern / climate change
- a natural disaster (this should be the general causes and effects rather than a specific event).

Suggest that they do Internet research if possible by typing key words into a search engine.

Tell them that the word limit should be 300 words and they should hand in a clear plan with their essay for marking.

CRITICAL THINKING SKILLS Assuming a causal link

This page helps students to evaluate the quality of evidence presented in a text.

If possible, do this *Critical thinking skills* page in class. Check that students understand the meaning of *assume* and *assumption,* and elicit the meaning of *jumping to conclusions.* Read through the examples with the students and encourage them to discuss each one in detail. Ask them what leads them to the conclusions about each.

Put the students into pairs or groups of three to discuss the causal links in each passage. Afterwards get them to compare ideas by joining another pair/group. Encourage them to give reasons for their answers.

As a follow-up, ask students: *What is the danger of jumping to conclusions in an academic context?*

ANSWER

Passage 1: The assumed causal link: obesity leads to longer life expectancy. The link does not follow logically from the reasons given: it hasn't been shown that those who are obese live longer, nor why obesity should lead to longer life.

Passage 2: The assumed causal link: that it was the roof-top protest that led to the prisoners' release, rather than, for example, them having been found innocent, the evidence against them being found to be flawed, or them having completed their sentences. Something which has happened only twice does not establish a solid trend.

Passage 3: The assumed causal links: that the man was murdered, that somebody broke in to do this, and that the knife was the murder weapon. However, in actuality, no murder may have occurred.

EXTENSION ACTIVITY

Ask students what a detective does (searches for and analyzes evidence in criminal investigations). Put students into groups. Ask them to discuss the answers to the following questions:

- What are the qualities of a good detective?
- What are the consequences if a detective "jumps to conclusions"?
- What should he/she do to ensure that this doesn't happen?
- Would you like to do this job? Why or why not?

UNIT 10 CONFLICT

Reading	Identifying causes
Critical thinking	Identifying humor
Language development	Phrasal nouns Verb patterns
Writing	The writer's voice

Ask students to look at the picture and say what they think it shows. Ask questions to stimulate ideas: *Do you know what these animals are? What are they doing? Why? What does the unit title, Conflict, mean? How do you think the picture relates to it?*

Background information

The picture shows two bull (male) northern elephant seals sparring. The majority of the population lives in colonies in the north east Pacific Ocean around California in the United States and Baja California in Mexico. In the breeding season, violent battles break out amongst the males as they compete for females. The resulting battles can endanger nearby females and young as well as ending in serious injury for the competing males.

Discussion point

To raise interest, ask the class whether this picture reminds them of human behavior. Elicit some examples, i.e., footballers squaring-up to each other following a collision or boxers looking each other in the eye to unnerve their opponent. Point out the colloquial expressions used to describe actions associated with anger and aggression.

EXTENSION ACTIVITY

If the students are interested, you could teach some more expressions related to conflict and anger, for example, *see red* (becoming very angry); *like a bear with a sore head* (describes someone who is bad-tempered/irritable); *bite someone's head off* (respond verbally in an aggressive manner); *take someone on* (get into a verbal or physical conflict). Ask if there are any similar expressions in their native language.

Put students into pairs or groups of three to discuss the questions. Monitor their discussions, encouraging them to expand their answers by giving examples and asking for further information. Afterwards, if your class doesn't usually mind sharing personal information, ask which approach in question 2 relates to them.

Vocabulary preview

Some of the words in the sentences may be new, so allow students to work in pairs to do the exercise if they wish. When checking the answers, ask students to say the full sentences and their matching definitions. Assist with pronunciation of new words where necessary.

ANSWERS

1 a	**5** a
2 c	**6** a
3 c	**7** b
4 c	**8** d

EXTENSION ACTIVITY

Put students into groups of three and ask them to make an example sentence with each word from sentences 1–8. Monitor and assist where necessary. Get confident students to read their examples to the class.

READING Culture and conflict

Word count 1,161

Background information

American anthropologist Edward T. Hall is well known amongst anthropologists for examining the concept of monochronic and polychronic time, or M-time and P-time, as he often called it. He was born in Missouri in 1914 and went on to study anthropology in several universities across the U.S. During the course of his career, he studied intercultural relations with many cultures including the Najavo, Hopi, Trukese, and Spanish-Americans. He published many academic papers and books, including *The Dance of Life: The Other Dimension of Time* and *The Hidden Dimension*, both of which explored cultures' differing perceptions of space and time. He died in 2009.

Before you read

As a lead-in, ask students: *Do you like doing chores? Why or why not?* Write the title of the reading, *Culture and conflict*, on the board and ask students what the text will be about. Write some of their ideas on the board and then put them into pairs to discuss the questions. Afterwards, ask some students to share their ideas with the class. Record any useful vocabulary that arises on the board.

Global reading

Exam tip

This exercise is similar to the summary completion tasks in the Academic IELTS Reading and Listening Tests, although the words are taken directly from the text instead of being synonyms as in IELTS. The teaching notes below review the strategies for successful completion of this type of task. Explain that like all skills, practice will make them faster, and more competent and confident in an exam situation, increasing the likelihood of a higher band score. Help these techniques become habitual to students by consistently reminding them to approach tasks using the appropriate strategies in all lessons. Always watch to see whether your exam students are using the skills and strategies that have been introduced in the book so far. It may be necessary to review some of these for consolidation.

1 Before beginning the exercise, ask students if they know the meaning of *humorous* (funny). Give students approximately two minutes to skim-read the text and then discuss the gist in pairs. Draw their attention to the words in the box above the summary.

Put students into pairs and label them *A* and *B*. Ask the As to find *diffuseness*, *high-context*, and *polychronic* in the text, and ask the Bs to find *low-context*, *monochronic*, and *specificity*. Give them a time limit of five minutes to scan for their words in the text and work out the meaning from context. Explain that they should be prepared to teach these words to their partner (A or B) afterwards. When they have finished, give further explanations as necessary, review the pronunciation, and elicit the parts of speech for each word: *diffuseness* (n), *high-context* (adj), *polychronic* (adj), *low-context* (adj), *monochronic* (adj), and *specificity* (n).

Elicit or explain the strategy for successful completion: read the summary carefully, focus on the words around the gaps, and then guess which part of speech (noun, verb, adjective, adverb, etc.) is required to fill each one. Then focus on the meaning required, especially if there is more than one example of each part of speech in the word box. Encourage students to also underline the key words in the summary before scanning for key words in the text. If your students are studying for their IELTS Test or equivalent, review the content of the *Exam tip* box above, reminding them that the exam will use synonyms. Ask students to do the exercise individually and then compare answers in pairs.

ANSWERS

1 low-context
2 high-context
3 polychronic
4 monochronic
5 diffuseness
6 specificity

Check that students remember the meaning of *infer* (to form an opinion about something that is based on information that you read / to suggest that something is true). Refer them to the *Identifying causes* box, and ask them to read though it and ask any necessary questions. Remind them that they studied cause and effect relationships in Unit 9, and suggest that they could refer back to it during independent study for consolidation.

2 Ask students to do the exercise individually. Remind them to underline key words in the scenarios so that they can scan for the corresponding parts of the text effectively. Tell them to annotate the text (writing the number of the question that is answered beside the correct part) so that they can refer back to it when discussing the answers during exercise 3.

POSSIBLE ANSWERS

1 The writer is a high-context communicator, but his wife has a low-context style. Because of this, he couldn't clearly communicate his concerns about the dishes to his wife.
2 The Asian businessman comes from a high-context culture where nonverbal communication and long silences are common, and he misinterprets the low-context American's direct communication style for rudeness.
3 The British woman is from a monochronic culture where schedules are very important, whereas her South American friend has a polychronic view of time and does not see arriving late as a sign of rudeness.
4 The Middle Eastern businessman has a polychronic view of time and sees it as natural to delay a meeting in order to help his family, whereas the European has a monochronic outlook that values schedules above relationships.

3 Put students into pairs or small groups to discuss the scenarios. When checking answers as a class, make sure they give full explanations, saying for example, *In scenario 2 where (an Asian businessman feels that an American has been rude to him) the main cause of the conflict is …*

ANSWERS

1 paragraph 3
2 paragraph 7
3 paragraph 9
4 paragraph 9

Draw students' attention to the *Academic keywords* box. Ask students if they know the meaning of the words and teach them if necessary. Review their pronunciation and stress, and tell students to add them to their vocabulary notebooks. If you are following the class wiki project, this unit's wiki group should also add these keywords to the wiki.

EXTENSION ACTIVITY

Put students into pairs or small groups. Ask them to think of situations where cultural differences cause difficulties in communication, for example, as in the text between people from monochronic and polychronic cultures.

They should choose two situations and prepare to explain them to the rest of the class. Write the following prompts on the board to help them:

- Describe the situation: who is involved?
- What action causes the misunderstanding?
- What are the effects of this?

Explain that they should aim to keep their descriptions clear and brief, lasting no longer than a minute. Afterwards, review some of the scenarios as a class and ask students how these situations could be avoided.

Critical thinking skill

Cultural awareness

Humor is very particular to culture, and you will probably already have noticed that your students tend to find quite different things amusing. The object of these exercises is to attempt to raise awareness of the different ways that writers use humor in English. Explain this to your students and tell them that it doesn't matter whether they get the humor or not. This is something that may (or may not) come with time and exposure to English.

SUPPORTING CRITICAL THINKING

This exercise requires students to identify and consider how the author uses different types of humor in the text. Some students may find this challenging (see the *Cultural awareness* box above) so allow plenty of time for pair and group discussion. It may help to discuss how humor is used in their native languages as a warmer before starting the exercise.

As a lead-in, ask students: *Do you find it easy to identify humor in English? Why or why not? Have you watched any comedy movies or series in English? Which ones? Did you find them funny?* Refer them to the *Identifying humor* box, and allow time for them to read it and ask you any questions. Check that they understand the meaning of *sarcasm*. Point out that sarcasm is relatively common in spoken English, but can be difficult to pick up on because it is suggested by the pitch of the voice and the context rather than the content of a statement.

1 Ask students to do the exercise individually and then discuss their answers in pairs. If they are having difficulties, ask them to join another pair to make groups of four. Check answers as a class.

ANSWERS

1, 2, 4, and 6 are meant to be humorous.

Developing critical thinking

SUPPORTING CRITICAL THINKING

Question 1 in this section requires the students to evaluate the way that they personally handle conflict with reference to the content of the text. Allow them a few minutes to take notes individually and consider how they will express themselves before putting them into groups to discuss the question. For question 2, students could organize their ideas in a table under the headings: *conflict; text;* and *other factors*. Again, give them time to develop their ideas before the discussion.

Put students into pairs or small groups for the discussion task. Monitor unobtrusively and listen to their discussions. Take note of any useful vocabulary or points to expand at the feedback stage. Remember to give positive feedback to help them gain confidence and provide extra incentive to try out new skills next time.

EXTENSION ACTIVITY

Ask students to brainstorm potential problems with communication between their culture and a different culture (English if it is different enough). Tell them to write a short text of two paragraphs (approximately 150 words) outlining:

- potential cultural misunderstandings (these could be body language/gestures; mono or polychronic differences or customs)
- key things that a foreign visitor could do to prepare for a trip to their country.

Afterwards, post them on the wall, and get the class to circulate and read. Ask students to take note of three things that they learned about another culture (if your class is mixed nationality), or three things that they read which they thought were important.

Language development: Phrasal nouns

As a lead-in, ask the class for some examples of phrasal verbs and their meanings (any will do just to get them interested). Draw their attention to the

Phrasal nouns box and ask if they know what a phrasal noun is. Give them time to read through the box and ask any necessary questions. Suggest that they keep a section in their vocabulary notebooks to record phrasal nouns.

1 Ask students to do exercise 1 in pairs. Suggest that they ask another pair if they're unsure about the meanings before consulting their monolingual dictionaries. Check their understanding by asking confident students to give definitions for the phrasal verbs.

2 Ask students to remain in their pairs to complete the sentences. Tell them to do this verbally first before filling the blanks. Point out the pronunciation of the words and elicit/explain that in most phrasal nouns, the stress is on the first syllable of the word. Ask them to say full sentences when checking the answers as a class.

ANSWERS
1 slowdown
2 build-up
3 outburst
4 breakup
5 drawback
6 runaround

3 Students discuss the questions in pairs or small groups. Again, ask students to give full sentences when they answer.

ANSWERS
Similar meanings: breakup, build-up, outburst, slowdown
Different meanings: drawback (verb = to move away from something; noun = disadvantage); runaround (verb = to run a circle around something; to be very busy doing different things; noun = a delay meant to evade or frustrate)
Different word order: outburst

4 Do this exercise in pairs or groups. Allow them plenty of time for the discussion, and encourage them to give reasons and examples, and to ask follow-up questions to extend it.

This is a good place to use the video resource *The warrior gene*. It is located in the Video resources section of the digital component. Alternatively, remind students about the video so they can view this at home. If you are following the class wiki project, this unit's wiki group can add some of the words from this section to the class wiki.

Language development: Verb patterns

At this level, students will already be familiar with a range of verb patterns, but they may not be using them correctly or consistently. This section gives them the chance to analyze them in more depth.

Explain that memorizing language in chunks such as verb patterns can be extremely useful for students as they can then use them confidently in their academic writing and when giving presentations. For consolidation, try to review verb patterns regularly in subsequent lessons and praise students when they use them correctly. Give students plenty of time to study the examples in the *Verb patterns* box and ask you questions if they need to. If time allows, put students into pairs and ask them to write an extra example sentence for each one given in the box. Afterwards, elicit some examples and write them on the board. Remind students that the sooner they use new phrases, the easier it is to retain them and use them again correctly.

1 As this is a productive exercise with a degree of cognitive challenge, give students plenty of time to complete it and allow them to discuss possible answers as they work. Encourage students to check the structure and prepositions which go with the verbs in a monolingual dictionary. Check answers as a class, making sure that students say the full sentences with the words in context.

ANSWERS
1 for hurting
2 about not being
3 someone to have
4 you to disagree
5 you of not listening
6 from criticizing
7 someone not to raise
8 someone for saying
9 from turning

2 Ask students to discuss the questions in pairs. Monitor and take note of any errors with verb patterns to feed back on afterwards. To avoid embarrassment or directly identifying students, write some examples for correction on the board (change the wording or topic of their wrong sentences slightly, but leave the error in place). Ask students to say how to correct the sentences. Get them to copy the corrected sentences into their notebooks as examples.

EXTENSION ACTIVITY

Ask students to find a text and "mine" the text for examples of each verb pattern. This could be done in class or for homework. Point out that they can do this in independent study with any text in order to improve their vocabulary and reading comprehension. The knowledge and skills gained from this type of activity can transfer to their own writing and speaking.

WRITING Analyzing a conflict

As a lead-in, ask students what they think *an author's voice* refers to. Elicit their ideas, and write any useful words and phrases on the board. Read through the instructions with the students and make sure that they understand the task.

Writing skill

Ask students to read the *The writer's voice* box and check whether their ideas about the meaning of *voice* were correct. Ask them to briefly recap the content of the box and ask concept questions to check comprehension if necessary.

1 Ask students to read the beginnings of the two essays and briefly tell you the gist of them. Ask them to discuss the questions in pairs and give them time to compare answers before checking as a class.

> **ANSWER**
> Voice 1 would be better for an essay in a magazine; voice 2 would be better for an academic paper. We know this because the language in voice 1 is less formal than in voice 2.

Elicit why students made their choices by asking questions such as: *Which words made you think that this style is more suited to a magazine?* (the use of haranguing and badgering is fairly colloquial, a higher number of verb phrases used, use of personal pronouns, informal style, descriptive vocabulary); *Why do you think this style is more academic?* (use of noun phrases, has a higher noun-verb ratio, use of essay statement *This essay will examine …* use of hedging language, passive construction, relative clauses, formal style).

2 Read through the instructions with the class and then focus on the voice options. Put students into groups of three and ask them to discuss the styles associated with each option. Review these before asking students to complete the task. Point out that they should try to rephrase the paragraphs in order to keep them a similar length. Allow plenty of time for the task. Monitor and assist when needed, taking note of any important points to feed back on.

3 Students compare and discuss their paragraphs. Encourage them to say which words show the style that they have used. As a follow-up, ask students whether writers use different voices in different types of writing in their language. If so, are there similarities and differences?

> **EXTENSION ACTIVITY**
> Bring in various short texts (or sections of texts) from a range of sources including magazines, newspapers, and academic journals. Put students into pairs or groups of three and give them two or three texts to analyze. Ask them to consider:
> - the type of text (magazine, newspaper, journal)
> - the author's voice (they should note down which words, phrases, or style features lead them to their conclusion)
> - the audience (who is the text targeted at and why?).

WRITING TASK

Refer students to the box at the top of the page which outlines the audience, context, and purpose. Read the essay instructions and make sure that students know what they are expected to do. Ask them to read the model text and then discuss the question in pairs. Elicit some of their ideas and write them on the board as a reminder as they write their essays.

> **ANSWERS**
> The American anthropologist Edward T. Hall's concept of monochronic and polychronic time is a valuable tool for understanding the deeper roots of intercultural conflict. A prime example of this can be found in the difficulties that a U.S. clothing company recently experienced while doing business in South America.
>
> The company initially came to the region with a very monochronic view of time, in which staying on schedule was more important than building relationships. In his first visit, the sales rep spent only a few days in the area. As a result, the trip caused him to feel anxious, as the people he met spent more time socializing than apparently doing business. In actuality, the South American partners saw socializing as part of business.
> The writer's voice is positive about using Hall's concept and critical of the company's approach to doing business in South America.

Brainstorm, plan, and write

Put students into pairs and ask them to make their lists for the *Brainstorm* section, or suggest mind maps if they prefer with the name of the conflicts as headwords and the causes as subsidiaries. Remind them that they could draw on some of the situations and causes from the
reading text.

Remind students how important it is to have a clear and logical plan in place before starting to write. Give them a time limit of ten minutes to do this and then put them into pairs to evaluate their plans. Monitor and advise where necessary, making sure that students are confident about moving on to the writing stage.

Do the writing task in class so that you can assist students where necessary and check that they are using their plans effectively. Tell them that they should write approximately 300 words, and remind them of the audience and context of their report. Set a time limit of approximately 40–60 minutes for the first draft.

Share, rewrite, and edit

Ask students to exchange their essays with a partner. Encourage them to use the Peer review checklist on page 109 when they are evaluating their partner's essays. Give students around ten minutes for this stage. Remind them to make constructive comments based on the checklist. Monitor and make sure that they number the parts of the essay that they want to comment on and then take notes on a separate piece of paper to share during feedback. The student whose work is being analyzed should respond by accepting, rejecting, or asking for further explanation and clarification. They can then write their own comments on their essay to help them when they rewrite.

Ask students to rewrite and edit the essay for homework unless they are studying for an academic exam, in which case, do it under timed conditions in class (it doesn't matter whether the essay mirrors an exam task—it should help your students to become accustomed to writing to a time limit). Encourage them to take into consideration their partner's feedback when rewriting. Remind them that they should provide a plan even for rewrites as this helps you assess how well they are organizing their ideas before writing. Use the photocopiable *Unit assignment checklist* on page 95 to assess the students' essays.

Extra research task

Ask students to research and prepare a short presentation of approximately one to one and a half minutes outlining an aspect of monochronic or polychronic culture. They can choose to focus on either monochronic or polychronic, giving a clear description of it including examples or compare the two in relation to ONE of the following: business or family relationships.

Allow students time to review and practice their presentations. Ask the audience to take notes so that they can summarize the main points afterwards, or to take note of at least two questions to ask at the end.

CRITICAL THINKING SKILLS Relevant and irrelevant evidence

This page helps students to evaluate evidence and decide whether it is relevant to a conclusion or not.

Cultural awareness

Whatever the nationality of your students, it is likely that academic writing in their native language has marked differences from English. They will have spent many years learning the structures and styles that are acceptable in their country's academic institutions, so learning and retaining how it is done in English is likely to present challenges. A good way to help your students gain confidence is to dedicate class time in which they can analyze and then experiment with writing. Emphasize that analysis of writing structure and techniques is a valuable part of their education and will stand them in good stead for success in an English-speaking college or university. Try to regularly review writing lessons as well as the *Study skills* and *Critical thinking skills* pages for consolidation.

If possible, do this *Critical thinking skills* page in class. Check that students understand the meaning of *relevant/relevance* and *irrelevant/irrelevance.* Read through the examples with the students and encourage them to discuss each one in detail. Ask them which words lead them to the conclusions about each.

For the *Check* section, tell students that memorizing this checklist will be valuable to them when checking their work. Meanwhile, they could keep a copy of it and refer to it in class. In writing lessons where it would be useful, write it on the board for reference.

EXTENSION ACTIVITY

Ask students to look back at the *How rivers made civilisation* text on page 90 and analyze the evidence presented in it. They should discuss in pairs or small groups whether they think it is used in the same way as example 1, 2, or 3 and say which words brought them to their conclusions. Alternatively, use a different text which gives evidence either from the textbook or another academic source.

UNIT 1 GATHERING

Student name: ______________________________

Date: ________________

Unit assignment: Writing an email

25 points: Excellent achievement. Student successfully fulfills the expectation for this part of the assignment with little or no room for improvement.

20 points: Good achievement. Student fulfills the expectation for this part of the assignment, but may have a few errors or need some improvement.

15 points: Satisfactory achievement. Student needs some work to fulfill the expectation for this part of the assignment, but shows some effort.

5 points: Poor achievement. Student does not fulfill the expectation for this part of the assignment.

	Met		**Unmet**		**Comments**
The email is around 100 words.					
The email is culturally acceptable and realistic in scope.					
	25 points	20 points	15 points	5 points	
The email uses an appropriate tone.					
The email begins and ends appropriately.					
The email uses appropriate verb forms.					
The email uses appropriate synonyms.					

Total points: ________ /100

Comments:

UNIT 2 GAMES

Student name: ______________________________

Date: ______________

Unit assignment: A compare and contrast report

25 points: Excellent achievement. Student successfully fulfills the expectation for this part of the assignment with little or no room for improvement.

20 points: Good achievement. Student fulfills the expectation for this part of the assignment, but may have a few errors or need some improvement.

15 points: Satisfactory achievement. Student needs some work to fulfill the expectation for this part of the assignment, but shows some effort.

5 points: Poor achievement. Student does not fulfill the expectation for this part of the assignment.

	Met		Unmet		Comments
The essay is around 300 words.					
The essay lists sources of information where appropriate.					
	25 points	20 points	15 points	5 points	
The essay compares and contrasts two host cities or countries.					
The essay includes recommendations.					
The essay follows the outline and is clearly organized.					
The essay uses expressions of contrast and appropriate vocabulary from the unit.					

Total points: ________ /100

Comments:

UNIT 3 NOSTALGIA

Student name: ______________________________

Date: ________________

Unit assignment: Analyzing a memory

25 points: Excellent achievement. Student successfully fulfills the expectation for this part of the assignment with little or no room for improvement.

20 points: Good achievement. Student fulfills the expectation for this part of the assignment, but may have a few errors or need some improvement.

15 points: Satisfactory achievement. Student needs some work to fulfill the expectation for this part of the assignment, but shows some effort.

5 points: Poor achievement. Student does not fulfill the expectation for this part of the assignment.

	Met		Unmet		Comments
The essay is around 300 words.					
The essay answers the assigned question.					
	25 points	20 points	15 points	5 points	
The essay is organized into paragraphs that follow the structure from the outline.					
The essay uses good transition sentences to link ideas between paragraphs.					
The essay uses reporting verbs to identify sources of information.					
The essay uses compound adjectives where appropriate.					

Total points: ________ /100

Comments:

UNIT 4 RISK

Student name: ______________________

Date: ______________

Unit assignment: Summary writing

25 points: Excellent achievement. Student successfully fulfills the expectation for this part of the assignment with little or no room for improvement.

20 points: Good achievement. Student fulfills the expectation for this part of the assignment, but may have a few errors or need some improvement.

15 points: Satisfactory achievement. Student needs some work to fulfill the expectation for this part of the assignment, but shows some effort.

5 points: Poor achievement. Student does not fulfill the expectation for this part of the assignment.

	Met		**Unmet**		**Comments**
The summary is around 300 words.					
	25 points	20 points	15 points	5 points	
The summary includes a thesis statement, key points, and supporting ideas.					
The writer has cited sources correctly.					
The writer has paraphrased and/or quoted appropriately.					
The writer uses adjective + preposition collocations and infinitive forms where appropriate.					

Total points: ________ /100

Comments:

UNIT 5 SPRAWL

Student name: ______________________________

Date: ________________

Unit assignment: An argumentative essay

25 points: Excellent achievement. Student successfully fulfills the expectation for this part of the assignment with little or no room for improvement.

20 points: Good achievement. Student fulfills the expectation for this part of the assignment, but may have a few errors or need some improvement.

15 points: Satisfactory achievement. Student needs some work to fulfill the expectation for this part of the assignment, but shows some effort.

5 points: Poor achievement. Student does not fulfill the expectation for this part of the assignment.

	Met		**Unmet**		**Comments**
The essay is around 300 words.					
It is clear what the writer's stance is on the topic.					
	25 points	20 points	15 points	5 points	
The essay presents a balanced viewpoint, including both advantages and drawbacks.					
The essay is well organized with good use of contrast words and transition sentences.					
The essay uses impersonal structures where appropriate.					
The essay uses hedging language and prepositional phrases where appropriate.					

Total points: ________ /100

Comments:

Student name: ______________________________

Date: ________________

Unit assignment: Describing changes

25 points: Excellent achievement. Student successfully fulfills the expectation for this part of the assignment with little or no room for improvement.

20 points: Good achievement. Student fulfills the expectation for this part of the assignment, but may have a few errors or need some improvement.

15 points: Satisfactory achievement. Student needs some work to fulfill the expectation for this part of the assignment, but shows some effort.

5 points: Poor achievement. Student does not fulfill the expectation for this part of the assignment.

	Met		**Unmet**		**Comments**
The essay is around 300 words.					
The essay answers the assigned question.					
	25 points	20 points	15 points	5 points	
The essay is organized into paragraphs that follow the structure from the outline.					
The essay includes a range of topic-related words with affixes.					
The essay uses some examples of relative pronouns with prepositions.					
The essay defines any scientific terms accurately.					

Total points: ________ /100

Comments:

UNIT 7 EXPANSE

Student name: ______________________________

Date: ______________

Unit assignment: A persuasive essay

25 points: Excellent achievement. Student successfully fulfills the expectation for this part of the assignment with little or no room for improvement.

20 points: Good achievement. Student fulfills the expectation for this part of the assignment, but may have a few errors or need some improvement.

15 points: Satisfactory achievement. Student needs some work to fulfill the expectation for this part of the assignment, but shows some effort.

5 points: Poor achievement. Student does not fulfill the expectation for this part of the assignment.

	Met		**Unmet**		**Comments**
The essay is around 300 words.					
The essay answers the assigned question.					
	25 points	20 points	15 points	5 points	
The essay is organized into paragraphs that follow the structure from the suggested plan.					
The essay includes some emphasizing phrases.					
The essay uses some persuasive techniques.					
The essay uses some adjective + noun collocations.					

Total points: ________ /100

Comments:

UNIT 8 CHANGE

Student name: ______________________

Date: ______________

Unit assignment: Report writing

25 points: Excellent achievement. Student successfully fulfills the expectation for this part of the assignment with little or no room for improvement.

20 points: Good achievement. Student fulfills the expectation for this part of the assignment, but may have a few errors or need some improvement.

15 points: Satisfactory achievement. Student needs some work to fulfill the expectation for this part of the assignment, but shows some effort.

5 points: Poor achievement. Student does not fulfill the expectation for this part of the assignment.

	Met		Unmet		Comments
The report is around 300 words.					
The report answers the assigned question.					
	25 points	20 points	15 points	5 points	
The report is organized into clear sections including an introduction, main body, and conclusion.					
The report outlines the writer's suggestions clearly and concisely.					
The report includes some examples of participle clauses.					
The report uses punctuation correctly.					

Total points: ________ /100

Comments:

UNIT 9 FLOW

Student name: ______________________________

Date: ________________

Unit assignment: A cause and effect essay

25 points: Excellent achievement. Student successfully fulfills the expectation for this part of the assignment with little or no room for improvement.

20 points: Good achievement. Student fulfills the expectation for this part of the assignment, but may have a few errors or need some improvement.

15 points: Satisfactory achievement. Student needs some work to fulfill the expectation for this part of the assignment, but shows some effort.

5 points: Poor achievement. Student does not fulfill the expectation for this part of the assignment.

	Met		**Unmet**		**Comments**
The essay is around 300 words.					
The essay answers the assigned question.					
	25 points	20 points	15 points	5 points	
The essay effectively outlines the cause and effect relationships between the geography, history, and culture of the place featured.					
The essay uses expressions of causality.					
The essay includes some verbs and expressions with prepositions.					
The essay uses punctuation correctly.					

Total points: ________ /100

Comments:

UNIT 10 CONFLICT

Student name: ______________________________

Date: ________________

Unit assignment: Analyzing a conflict

25 points: Excellent achievement. Student successfully fulfills the expectation for this part of the assignment with little or no room for improvement.

20 points: Good achievement. Student fulfills the expectation for this part of the assignment, but may have a few errors or need some improvement.

15 points: Satisfactory achievement. Student needs some work to fulfill the expectation for this part of the assignment, but shows some effort.

5 points: Poor achievement. Student does not fulfill the expectation for this part of the assignment.

	Met		**Unmet**		**Comments**
The essay is around 300 words.					
The essay answers the assigned question.					
	25 points	20 points	15 points	5 points	
The essay describes the best way to resolve a conflict.					
The essay uses an example / examples of phrasal nouns.					
The essay uses a range of verb patterns.					
The essay uses punctuation correctly.					

Total points: ________ /100

Comments:

UNIT 1 Gathering

Vocabulary preview

1 people you know 2 evidence based on observation 3 different 4 develops
5 someone who is interested only in him/herself 6 connections 7 children who are changing into young adults
8 help to develop 9 always linked to people via technology 10 ability to understand how someone feels

READING Are online "friends" a threat to development?

Global reading

3

Writer's position = 2, 4

Critical thinking skill

1

1 The impact of technology on the nature of our friendships has been a much-debated topic since the meteoric rise of social networks.
2 In fact there is a lot of research that shows these criticisms are generally unfounded.
3 They also found that social networks allow us to have discussions with a much more diverse set of people than in the real world, so we share knowledge with people from a wide variety of backgrounds.
4 A study conducted by Michigan State University (2010) concluded that our virtual friendships provide social benefits and improve our psychological well-being.
5 Research is starting to show that this culture is negatively affecting not our friendships but our character.
6 Through her years of research, she has noticed that these devices permit us to have complete control over our friendships.
7 Friendships are unpredictable and difficult to deal with, but social networks are allowing people to tidy them up and manage them.
8 Turkle also suggests that people are no longer comfortable being alone.

2

1 d	2 a	3 a	4 f
5 c	6 d	7 e	8 b & e

3

1 and 6 are not arguments because the statements are not supported by evidence/reasons.

Language development: Synonyms

1

1 i 2 h 3 a 4 f 5 g 6 d 7 e 8 b 9 c 10 j

Provide and *permit* are all slightly more formal than their synonyms; *adolescents* are people going through puberty so could be younger than 13, when teenage years traditionally start; *deal with* is just one sense of "manage"; you *nurture* a child, animal, or plant, but you can *foster* many other things, e.g., understanding, a feeling of happiness.

2

Possible answers:

1 adolescents; worried; impact; society/planet
2 uncommon; virtual; ties/links
3 allows; form/create; relationships; diverse
4 unfounded; reduction/drop; face-to-face
5 character; appear; evolving
6 alone; get in touch with

3

Possible answers:

The human brain is constantly changing, and neuroscientist Gary Small believes it is evolving further because of new technologies. He believes that our ability to multitask is improving. He says that our skills in making decisions are getting better. He also suggests that technology is developing our decision-making abilities. One study carried out with people aged between 55 and 76 using the Internet showed that the brains of the people who could already use the web displayed much greater activity than those of the people who could not already use it.

Language development: Simple and progressive verb forms

1

1 The simple forms all describe completed actions. The progressive forms are all used to describe duration (*had been chatting, will be chatting*) or incompletion (*have been using*).

2&3

1 have been carrying out
2 has shown
3 has helped
4 has taken
5 had benefited
6 had used
7 had then replied
8 had been lacking
9 had begun
10 will be adopting

WRITING Writing an email

Writing skill

1

1 Formal/Academic: writer to reader (formal language, e.g., *It is said that;* no contractions; *an increase in online communication,* i.e., noun phrase)
2 Formal: company to customer (formal, polite language, *product;* no contractions; no abbreviations, e.g., *ASAP*)
3 Informal: colleagues (friendly, chatty style; contractions; slang, e.g., *gonna;* phrasal verbs; abbreviations)
4 Neutral: student to professor he or she is acquainted with (polite but friendly; contractions; phrasal verbs but no slang)

2

1 Could you call me as soon as you can? I have a problem I can't deal with and need your help.
2 I'm very concerned that I won't be able to do my assignment in time and you won't be able to pass it. Is it possible for me to have an extension?
3 I'm Ahmed's friend. Ahmed suggested that you could help me with my research. Do you think that is possible?
4 I'm attaching a copy of my finished assignment, which I hope you enjoy. See you in class next week.

WRITING TASK

Possible answer:

Hi Joelle,
How are you? How was your weekend? Mine was hectic as usual!
Are you free later this week to get together and chat about the psychology project? I've been struggling with it and need a bit of help cos the deadline's fast approaching. I'm worried that if I don't get a move on, I'll end up rushing it. I really want to get a good grade for this one so need to put some work in.
How about tomorrow night? I've got an appointment in the afternoon but I'll be done by 6pm. Does 7pm sound okay? I can come to you if it's easier. I could even bring pizza if you like. Let me know asap.
Hopefully see you soon,
Allie

Brainstorm

Tone—friendly but more polite and less chatty
Language—less slang and more neutral language, fewer phrasal verbs and abbreviations
Punctuation—no exclamation marks

STUDY SKILLS Process writing and peer checking

Scenario

Possible answer:

Saif read the question carefully, he did lots of research, and he emailed his work to his teacher with a friendly, polite email. However, he spent only two hours writing the essay, he did not organize his work effectively, he did not ask a classmate to peer check it, and he gave his classmate only negative feedback.

UNIT 2 Games

Vocabulary preview

1 surplus 2 budget 3 financial 4 debt
5 gross domestic product (GDP) 6 return
7 exceeded 8 revenue

READING After the Games end: Risks and rewards of hosting the Olympics®

Global reading

1

b

2

1 Both cities 2 Barcelona 3 Athens 4 Athens
5 Athens 6 Both cities

Critical thinking skill

1

The three main arguments are 1, 3, and 4.

2 is not correct. The report argues that private businesses need to cooperate with public entities.

5 is not correct. The report argues the opposite, that increased prestige leads to more revenue from increased tourism and trade.

2

1 Starting around 2008, many countries in the European Union had high levels of debt, including Greece.
2 "The chance to bring the Games back to their historic roots" refers to the fact that the Olympic Games originally began in ancient Greece.
3 "The events of September 2001" refers to the September 11th terrorist attacks in New York City and Washington, D.C.

3

1 No. The paper mentions "our better-known neighbours on the east coast." It is not clear which city this refers to, but we can infer that the city in the report is not as well known.
2 No. The paper says, "In this city, where a single sport captures most people's attention, there may be little long-term return on the investment in these venues." We do not know exactly what the "single sport" is, but we can infer it is not one for which a new venue is needed.
3 Yes. The paper refers to "the city's recent experience with the expansion of the art museum" as "an excellent base for cooperation."
4 It is most likely a rainy city or one with other sorts of weather that can delay events. The paper says, "Similarly, any city with weather like ours ought to plan for delays in events that are held outdoors."

Language development: Guessing meaning from context

1

1 overview **2** benefits **3** costs **4** prestige
5 exports **6** less popular

2

1 b **2** d **3** a **4** c

3

Possible answers:

account: a record
risks: dangers or problems
confers: gives an honour to
boosting: helping something to increase
obscure: not well known
substantial: large or considerable
massive: very large
soared: increased very quickly
stakeholders: the people and groups with an interest in a project

4

Possible answers:

outcomes: final results of a project
partnership: the relationship between groups involved in a project together
showcase: to show something in a way that emphasizes its good qualities

Language development: Expressing contrast

1

1 In contrast to **2** however **3** However,
4 though **5** In contrast, **6** Despite **7** Unlike

WRITING A compare and contrast report

Writing skill

ii 1 c 2 e   iii 1 a 2 d, b   iv f

WRITING TASK

a is covered; b needs to be added to the outline

STUDY SKILLS Finding an idea to write about

Scenario

Possible answer:

Hassan could have conducted more research and compiled notes before writing his essay. He also didn't stick to the essay title assigned by the teacher.

UNIT 3 Nostalgia

Vocabulary preview

1

1 recall **2** eyewitnesses; stable
3 hippocampus **4** perceptions **5** short-term
6 long-term **7** neuroscientists

READING The shifting sands of memory

Global reading

1

c

2

Analogies mentioned: 1, 3, 4

3

Possible answers:

1 Memory is like a video recorder because it captures everything we see and hear with perfect accuracy.
3 Memory is like a computer's hard drive because it stores and preserves memories complete and intact.
4 Memory is like a recipe because you recreate it each time you recall it, using different "ingredients" such as sights, smells, sounds. In addition, there are opportunities for error when following a recipe, and in the same way a memory can be distorted over time.

4

4 The author believes the recipe is the best analogy because it explains how a single memory is a collection of separate pieces or "ingredients" and why our memories can sometimes be inaccurate.

5

Statements 2, 4, and 5 are true.

1 False. No one can recall being a baby because the part of the brain that forms these recollections takes a year to develop.
3 False. The hippocampus decides what to remember, but the memories are stored in many different parts of the brain.
6 False. Long-term memories often disappear or have serious inaccuracies.
7 False. However, they have done studies on drugs that help people forget things.

Critical thinking skill

1

1 the writer's mother
2 Elizabeth Loftus, a professor of psychology at the University of California
3 no source given; it's the author's own claim
4 Marc Green, an expert on memory and witness testimony
5 studies on memory show this; author does not say which studies
6 Karim Nader, a neuroscientist at McGill University
7 "other studies"—the author does not say which ones

2

Possible answers:

"the results were dry and disappointing" (para. 2): the author's own opinion and experience
"25% of the subjects claimed that they clearly remembered the false incident" (para. 4): a well-known experiment by Elizabeth Loftus
"childhood memories have profound and long-lasting effects on our relationships with our family, friends, and spouses." (para. 5): no source given
"a tiny seahorse-shaped structure in the brain called the hippocampus plays a crucial role in deciding which events are worth saving as long-term memories." (para. 8): the author cites "researchers" but doesn't name specific ones
"a drug called propranolol reduced the intensity of traumatic memories of war and violence." (para. 10): a later experiment
"Loftus and her colleagues explain how they convinced subjects that they loved to eat asparagus as children." (para. 12): a study by Loftus called "Healthier Eating Could Be Just a False Memory Away"

3

1 Answers will vary, but the most reliable information in exercise 1 is probably 2, 4, and 6 since their sources are experts in the study of memory and the brain. Information that is not sourced as completely (e.g., 5 and 7) may be less credible. Item 3 has no source but is probably true simply based on common sense.
2 You would usually not expect to find the writer's mother or the writer's own claims and memories used as sources in news articles or in academic essays on scientific subjects such as this one. In addition, in an academic essay the writer would specify which studies (not simply "other studies") support her claims.

Language development: Reporting information

1

neutral: explain, say
has been proven: conclude, demonstrate, find, learn, show, state
has not been proven: argue, assume, believe, claim, indicate, suggest,

2

1 claims (because the report "offers no evidence")
2 found (because it is a "convincing" study)
3 argued; suggested (because the sentence implies that none of the studies have settled the issue)

4 concluded (because *believe* is used with people, not with studies)
5 show (because *learn* is used with people, not with data)
6 shows (because it goes with the adverb *clearly*)

3

Possible answers:

1 According to the report, memory is reliable.
2 In fact, doing crossword puzzles improves people's memory.
3 The effect of caffeine on memory is still unclear; according to some studies, it has a positive effect, but according to others, this isn't true.
4 According to a recent experiment in Indonesia, elderly people who eat a great deal of tofu have a higher risk of memory loss.
5 In fact, a diet high in fish is good for people's memory.
6 In fact, people with long-term back or neck pain often have trouble remembering things.

Language development: Condensing information with compound adjectives

1

1 well-paid 2 heartbreaking; hard-working
3 pink-haired; brightly colored
4 smooth-talking 5 record-breaking
6 densely populated

2

1 Jane is a strong-willed person who rarely changes her mind.
2 Painful memories are often the cause of deep-rooted problems.
3 It's easy to remember Todd Splodd because of his odd-sounding name.
4 Because Jim is an open-minded person, he is always learning new things.
5 This is a never-ending documentary! When will it be over?
6 To remember the prefix *tri-*, think of a triangle or a tricycle, which is a three-wheeled bicycle.

WRITING Analyzing a memory

Writing skill

1

1 b 2 d 3 c

WRITING TASK

Although memories are generally reliable, research and personal experience both suggest that childhood memories are often less accurate. According to one well-known study by memory expert Elizabeth Loftus, up to 25% of subjects can have vivid, but false, memories of events that never happened to them. These findings are reflected in some of my own recollections. In one of my earliest memories, my mother fell asleep while we were coming home from school on a city bus. I remember being truly frightened. Would we miss our stop? Luckily, she woke up in time. According to my mother, this memory is false. She says there were no bus routes near my school, and she found a long-forgotten bus map that demonstrated this fact. She also claims that she may have appeared to be asleep on another bus trip, but was only "resting her eyes."
These inaccuracies show how early memories can be distorted. Some details are likely to be true, while others are simply false, and perceptions from different times and events may have combined to form a single memory.

UNIT 4 Risk

Vocabulary preview

1 seek
2 disregard
3 consequences
4 personality trait
5 biological makeup
6 susceptibility
7 sound judgment
8 peer pressure

READING Risk-takers: Who are they?

Global reading

1

2, 3, 4, 6

2

Possible answers:

Biological reasons: dopamine—physical reason for risk-taking: neurotransmitter, linked to brain's reward system, people with fewer dopamine receptors = flooded cell = feeling of extreme happiness, research 34 men and women = questionnaire and brain scan found people with fewer dopamine receptors are risk-takers
Psychological reasons: sensation-seeking scale—psychological reason for risk-taking, Zuckerman's scale—40-item questionnaire to identify sensation-seeking people who are more likely to take risks, twin study showed 60% of sensation-seeking trait is genetic
Age: Giedd (NIMH, U.S.) study of brain scans 145 children every two years over ten years—results showed pre-frontal cortex (controls planning, judgment, reason) undeveloped until age 25—young people more likely to take risks
Gender: research Columbia Business School, U.S.—gender affects type of risk-taking—men take financial risks, and women take social risks, men and women seem to perceive risk differently

3

The most appropriate is 2. 1 and 3 do not cover all the ideas in the paper.

Critical thinking skill

1

1 study at Vanderbilt University and Albert Einstein College of Medicine
2 Marvin Zuckerman's sensation-seeking scale
3 Zuckerman's twin study
4 National Institute of Mental Health, U.S., study
5 Columbia Business School research
6 Columbia Business School research

2

Possible answers

1 The sample is fairly substantial; it involved brain scanning, which can be considered objective; similar studies and results were seen in rats.
2 It was carried out by a respected psychologist; based on research with different types of people. Although not necessarily up-to-date, the scale is still used today.
3 The research was conducted with two types of identical twins and compared to research regarding other traits.
4 It was conducted by an official institution (U.S. National Institute of Mental Health).
5 The research has been done recently (2011) and therefore has currency. It supports the topic and gives reasons as to why people take risks. It is therefore relevant to the paper.

Language development: Adjective + preposition collocations

1

1 in	2 on	3 of	4 with
5 with	6 in	7 to	8 to
9 of	10 to	11 for	12 in

Language development: Infinitive phrases

1

1 Sentence 1 refers to the present (habit) and sentence 2 refers to the past.
2 Sentence 1 refers to the present (in progress) and sentence 2 refers to the past.
3 Sentence 1 refers to the present (habit) and sentence 2 refers to the past.
4 Sentence 1 is active and sentence 2 is passive; both use present perfect.

2

1 to be protecting
2 be given
3 to have learned
4 be needed
5 to be missing out
6 to have enjoyed

WRITING Summary writing

Writing skill

1

The topic is peer pressure and its effect on teenage drivers.

2

Main argument: Peer pressure affects teenage drivers, which may explain the higher number of accidents among teenagers.
Supporting argument: In a study, teenagers showed that they were willing to take more risks when they thought friends were watching.
Student's own ideas for the thesis statement.

3

The writer is not sourced; there is no date of the author's work; much of the text is copied and not paraphrased; the study is not named, dated, or sourced.

4

Possible answer:

Dr. Bauman (2013) suggests that teenage drivers may be influenced by pressure from friends. A Temple University study found that teenagers playing a computer driving game were more likely to take risks when they thought that same-sex friends were watching them, explaining why more accidents are caused by teenagers than other age groups.

WRITING TASK

In her article "The need to learn risk" (2013), which can be found in the *Journal of Risk Literacy* (Vol. 2, Issue 4), Patricia Hughes argues that risk literacy is essential in our daily lives and therefore should be studied in schools in order to help young people to calculate risk better, suggesting ways in which risk literacy could be taught. To support her argument, Hughes provides evidence that risk literacy education has been successful among 16-year-olds. One hundred 16-year-olds were involved in her study, which required them to make decisions about how to save or invest money both prior and subsequent to receiving lessons on statistics. The teenagers appeared to have been more successful in making decisions based on calculated risk after their lessons, which prompted Hughes to say that "secondary schools should be doing more to teach risk literacy in math lessons."

Yes, it has been sourced appropriately.

Brainstorm

Step 1: Skim-read the text.

Step 2: Reread the text carefully and take notes.

Step 3: Write a thesis statement.

Step 4: Write the summary using your own words. Include a thesis statement plus supporting ideas.

Write

Possible answer:

Wittman (2012) believes that age, gender, character, brain, and genetic makeup can all help to determine whether a person is a risk-taker.

A joint study at Vanderbilt University and Albert Einstein College of Medicine demonstrated that the chemical associated with pleasure in our brains can impact on risk-taking activities. People whose brain cells had fewer active dopamine receptors were bigger risk-takers. As the receptors are unable to prevent a cell from becoming flooded with dopamine, a strong feeling of excitement is felt. It is therefore likely that people with fewer active receptors try to repeat this feeling by taking more risks.

The pre-frontal cortex part of the brain may also impact on risk-taking activities. This is the part of our brain that deals with reason. Research carried out at the National Institute of Mental Health showed that it may not fully form until a person is 25. This may affect a person's judgment and cause him or her to take more risks.

Our personalities may also be a factor in risk-taking. In the 1960s, Marvin Zuckerman identified the sensation-seeking personality trait. In research with identical twins, he found that 60% of this trait is inherited. As with dopamine, people who are sensation-seekers may take more risks as they attempt to find new and exciting activities.

Finally, the types of risk that a person takes may be affected by gender. Research by Columbia Business School suggests that men are more likely to take financial risks, whereas women tend to take social risks. The researchers also claim that risk is perceived differently depending on a person's life experience and that this may be affected by gender.

Although Wittman does not identify one specific cause of risk-taking, all of the research above indicates that there could be a number of causes.

STUDY SKILLS Evaluating online sources

Scenario

Possible answer:

Liliana accessed academic websites; she made notes as she did her research and recorded the web addresses so she could find/source them later; and she sourced the work in her essay. However, she looked only at the first ten websites she found; she looked only for information that supported her point of view; and when she wrote her essay, she presented just one argument. Finally, not all her supporting information was valid and reliable. She did not know where all the information came from, and the information presented by the road safety campaign website may be biased.

UNIT 5 Sprawl

Vocabulary preview

1 c **2** g **3** d **4** a **5** f **6** e **7** h **8** b

READING Solving the problem of informal settlements

Global reading

1

Rehousing people means taking them away from their existing community and giving them housing in a different area. Upgrading settlements involves trying to improve people's existing housing and community.

2

residents, government, middle-class families, youth, nearby city residents, NGOs, Mumbai citizens

3

	Rehousing	Settlement upgrading
Informal community residents	better economic situation / access to services such as water, etc.	keep in touch with the community / more work opportunities / cheaper rent
Governments	reclaim land / bring residents into the mainstream —pay taxes	more economically viable / less money is spent on infrastructure
Other city residents	own house value no longer affected	would retain the benefits of having nearby existing dwellers offering services such as recycling
NGOs	affects psychological health of residents	build on community spirit and informal economies

4

1 B **2** U **3** B **4** R **5** R **6** B

Critical thinking skill

1

1 five billion, 3.3 billion **2** Nearly one billion **3** 500 million **4** 60 **5** 80 **6** Around 85 **7** 700 million **8** two billion

2

1, 3, and 8 are trends; 4 is a pattern. The others are static figures.

Language development: Prepositional phrases

2

1. On the face of it (used to introduce something that appears to be true but may not be when closely examined)
2. by no means (emphasizes a negative statement)
3. in response to (in answer to)
4. In terms of (in relation to / with reference to)
5. in favor of (support an idea)
6. In the event of (used to say what will happen in a future situation)
7. on the increase (increasing)
8. In light of (because of)

3

1 d **2** c **3** a **4** e **5** b

Language development: Impersonal report structures

1

1. It is known that people are unable to find work in rural areas.
2. Living in a city is supposed to bring more employment opportunities (for people).
3. There is thought to be greater access to schooling.
4. It is believed that transport is much better in the city.
5. There are estimated to be 70 million people moving to cities each year.
6. Urban life is alleged to be worse for migrants (by some people).
7. It is claimed that this is not true and rural life is far worse.
8. Urbanization is said to be necessary for a country to develop.

WRITING An argumentative essay

Writing skill

1

1 Generally (adverb of probability) / indicates (verb)
2 appear (verb) / are likely to (adverb of probability)
3 tend to be (verb) / suggests (verb)
4 In some cases (determiner) / may (modal)

2

The writer presents the information as fact. However, as none of the ideas in the text are supported by empirical evidence, it would be better for the writer to use some hedging language.

WRITING TASK

The key advantage of slum tourism is thought to be the understanding that tourists gain about the complexities of life in an informal settlement. Visitors can learn not only about the problems that exist within these communities, but also about the supportive community within which the residents live. This could lead to a greater understanding of how society should work together to develop these areas and improve living standards. On the other hand, it is believed that some visitors are not interested in understanding the issues but are instead visiting out of a sense of curiosity. This is unlikely to result in any kind of long-term advantage for the people that agree to be observed, and suggests that these tours are not helpful.

Brainstorm

Possible answers:

	Advantages	Disadvantages
The tourists	better cultural understanding	-
The residents	work with tour company; tourists may give money to help improve their lives	treated like a tourist attraction, like a zoo; tour companies may not employ local residents; residents are watched by people in expensive clothes with expensive accessories/ equipment
The tour company	makes a profit; may help the community; generates cultural understanding	damages their reputation among customers of other products who do not like this venture
Society as a whole	educates people and raises awareness, which can reduce poverty; in long-term, people more motivated to improve living conditions	creates a greater and more obvious social divide

UNIT 6 Legacy

Vocabulary preview

1 Endangered
2 ethnic groups
3 extinction
4 linguist
5 document
6 tongue
7 revitalize
8 native language

READING Endangered languages: Strategies for preservation and revitalization

Before you read

1 7,000 2 40% 3 1%

Global reading

1

1 When and why languages become endangered
2 When and why languages become endangered
3 Endangered languages on the rise
4 Revitalization efforts
5 Why endangered languages matter

2

Possible answers:

1 Languages become endangered due to a number of factors, including globalization, economics, technology, education policy, and changes in cultural attitudes.
2 A language is considered endangered when it has fewer than 1,000 native speakers who make up about half of the language's community; when only some parents speak the language at home; when few of those parents teach the language at home; and when it is not used in schools or for official business.
3 More than 40% of the world's 7,000 languages are endangered (roughly 2,800 languages in total).
4 Efforts to save endangered languages focus on two main areas: the documentation of endangered languages and efforts to increase the use of endangered languages in the community.
5 When a language becomes extinct, oral literature, historical knowledge, and knowledge of the natural world and local environment may all be lost, among other things.

Critical thinking skill

1

1 fact 2 speculation 3 fact 4 opinion
5 speculation 6 opinion

2

1 Not supported—Catalogue of Endangered Languages says only about 40% of languages are endangered.
2 Supported—Supporting facts may vary.
3 Not supported—The paper gives examples of languages that have been helped, but does not offer any facts supporting or refuting the idea that these efforts are futile.

Language development: Words with more than one affix

1

1 revitalize
2 popularization
3 endangerment
4 Globalization
5 validation
6 revitalization
7 disappearance
8 classification

Language development: Relative pronouns with prepositions

1 of which 2 in which 3 of which
4 with whom 5 in which 6 of which
7 for which 8 in which

WRITING Describing changes

Writing skill

1

Possible answers:

1 *Pisan zapra* is a Malay word that refers to the length of time needed to eat a banana.
2 The act of tiptoeing over warm sand is called *hanyauku* in the Kwangali language.
3 The Scottish word *tartle* is defined as "to hesitate while introducing a person because you can't remember his/her name."
4 A joke that is so unfunny and badly told that a person can't help but laugh is referred to as a *jayus in* the Indonesian language.
5 *Mokita* is a word in the Kilivila language that means something we all know but agree not to talk about.
6 In the Rapa Nui language, *tingo* is a term for stealing all of your neighbor's possessions by gradually borrowing them one by one.

WRITING TASK

Possible answer:

An endangered language has been defined in the Catalogue of Endangered Languages as one in which there are fewer than 1,000 speakers. Two such endangered languages are the Siletz language spoken in the northwestern part of the United States, and Koro, a language of northeast India. Of the two, Siletz is, with only five remaining elderly speakers, the most endangered language, whilst the fact that Koro has some 800 native speakers, around two-thirds of the total population, gives some ground for hope that it can be saved. Yet hopefulness alone cannot save a language from becoming extinct. There are encouraging signs that Siletz is being revitalized through local government and tribal support for initiatives such as classes, online dictionaries, and use of the language in documents. However, given that the language is currently only rarely used at home, and is generally restricted to use in tribal ceremonies, the issue remains one in which non-native speakers within the tribe may well feel that its reintroduction at this stage is already too late to save it as a living language in the face of globalization, and the cultural and linguistic impact that this brings. The recognition that it is extremely endangered is possibly the greatest advantage that those striving to preserve the language have.

In contrast, there is relatively little data available concerning the Koro language; a language which was not known about beyond the immediate community until 2010. The fact that its use is as a second language for the majority of its speakers, and that it is used only at home makes it more difficult to gather sufficient data to draw up a strategy for repopularizing it. Videos to document the language will help. With Koro, though there is at least an opportunity to recognize and respond to the crisis. For Siletz, the writing may be in the online dictionary, but it looks increasingly unlikely that it can be saved as a living language.

STUDY SKILLS Academic referencing

Getting started

1 bibliography: a list of the books, articles, etc. that someone has used for finding information for a piece of work they have written
citation: a phrase or sentence taken from a piece of writing or speech
credits: acknowledgement for something people have done or achieved
index: an alphabetical list of something such as subjects or names at the back of a book that shows on which page they are mentioned
reference (list): a writer or a piece of work that is mentioned in a piece of writing by someone else
2 family name of the author and date of publication
3 authors, date, title of academic paper, conference details, page numbers
authors, date, title of academic paper, full URL, date accessed

Scenario

Possible answer:

Julia sounds like she is a dedicated student; taking notes, summarizing, and paraphrasing. She is also careful to list source references. However, she is not having so much success with her term papers or essays as compared to previously. There is something different in her transition from engineering to psychology. These subjects are very different, with one being math based and the other social science based. It may well be that she is not adapting to the change in style of writing needed for psychology. Another factor could be simply that her tutor grades more harshly. There could also be another factor to do with essay styles, as hinted by the mention of source references.

UNIT 7 Expanse

Vocabulary preview

1 there is not much of something
2 placing pressure on
3 using a part of something
4 energy sources that are replaced naturally and never used up
5 methods that do not harm the environment
6 a large area of buildings, etc., that have spread from a city into the countryside, usually in an unattractive way
7 bring water to land to grow crops
8 ceased to exist
9 the process by which earth is removed by rain, wind, or the sea
10 very successful
11 the variety of different types of plants and animals that live in a region
12 a situation that is the worst you can imagine

READING Overpopulation: A problem or a myth?

Global reading

1

Possible answers:

Overpopulation: a problem

- We are placing enormous pressure on the Earth. If this increased, it could have a profound and irreversible effect.
- There's an existing shortage of water. By 2030 the UN estimates we'll need 30% more. Without sufficient water there will be health problems, and our food and manufacturing industries will be unable to meet demand.
- Current agricultural practices, pollution, deforestation, and mining are already degrading land and impacting on our ecosystem. Increases in population will create food instability. By 2030 the UN estimates we'll need 50% more food.
- Energy use is likely to rise. The UN estimates that we'll need 45% more energy by 2030. Rising oil costs will drive people into poverty.

Overpopulation: a myth

- Population predictions are usually incorrect. The population increase is likely to be far lower as family sizes continue to reduce. The average woman now has 2.5 children, only slightly higher than the 2.3 replacement rate.
- The main problems with food, water, and space are not the result of a lack of supply, but the way it is distributed.
- Crop yields could be increased.
- The threat comes from an imbalanced and unsustainable increase in consumption. 80% of the world's resources are consumed by 20% of the population according to the UN.
- What is needed is a focus on education against materialism and consumption rather than a focus on the wrong issues—to do otherwise would mean that the planet could not sustain human life.

2

Argument A: A problem

Repetition for emphasis Paragraph 1: the same number of people who currently live in the African and American continents combined; **Future insights** Paragraph 2: That is more than twice the number of people we have today. Paragraph 3: Without clean drinking water, there will be a rapid rise in diseases … / This is likely to increase … Paragraph 5: It is therefore likely that there will be a higher demand for oil … / This will make it more difficult … ; **Questions** Paragraph 4: How can we allow this destruction to occur under our noses …? Paragraph 6: Who can argue with free and equal education for everyone?

Argument B: A myth

Repetition for emphasis Paragraph 4: … which means that a fifth of us use four-fifths of the world's food and energy; **Future insights** Paragraph 2: … it is the low variant that has come true in the past, suggesting the same will be true of their future population predictions. Paragraph 5: … we may find ourselves living on a planet that can no longer sustain human life.; **Dismissing alternative arguments** Paragraph 3: … Raj Krishna estimates that India alone is capable of increasing crop yields to the point of providing the entire world's food supply. / There is the same amount of fresh water on the planet now as there was 10,000 years ago; **Emotional vocabulary** Paragraph 4: sad truth; Paragraph 5: horrendous

Critical thinking skill

1

a trend **b** static figure **c** static figure
d pattern **e** static figure **f** trend

2

Possible answer:

Dr. Rice is illustrating that the problem of overpopulation is increasing / getting worse.

3

1 no (even though the text suggests this, the use of *will* is too strong)
2 no (even though the text suggests this, the use of *will* is too strong)
3 yes (there is evidence of the negative effects of deforestation and mining)
4 yes (statistics support it)
5 yes and no (education is likely to be one of a number of solutions)
6 no (if there is a finite amount of water, then logically a higher population will put more strain on this amount)
7 no (this is a generalization which is unlikely)
8 yes (we can see plenty of evidence of waste, and there will be statistics available)
9 no (even though the text suggests this, the use of *will* is too strong)
10 no (even though the text suggests this, the use of *will* is too strong)

4

Possible answer:

Dr. Rice has the better and more logical arguments as they are supported by evidence; the research is valid and reliable, and supports the conclusions. Marilyn Cratchley's text is not a good academic model. She does not support her arguments with effective points, and they do not all support the conclusions.

Language development: Adjective + noun collocations

1

1 enormous **2** profound **3** major **4** rapid **5** greater **6** prime **7** huge **8** greater **9** higher **10** bigger

2

1 a considerable **b** widespread **c** systematic
2 a substantial **b** crucial **c** prominent
3 a principal **b** acute **c** leading

Language development: Noun (nominal) clauses

1

1 they can follow fashion without spending much
2 that fast fashion affects the environment
3 that polyester is made from petroleum
4 What may result from this
5 How cotton is grown
6 whether they need new clothes or not

2

1 that **2** that **3** How/Where **4** that **5** What **6** if/whether

WRITING A persuasive essay

Writing skill

1

1 Only when humans started to grow crops and keep farm animals did the world population begin to increase more quickly.
2 What many people do not realize is that our world cannot continue to sustain our needs.
3 Rarely do world leaders discuss the issue of overpopulation.
4 It is governments that should address the issue of world poverty. / It is the issue of world poverty that governments should address.
5 Not only does education help people escape poverty, it also helps them understand global issues.
6 It is men who are more likely to be educated than women.
7 It is now that we should address these issues and not in the future.

4

1 it is the ability to read and write that affects your life the most
2 Rarely do you
3 it does make
4 What you have to do is rely on other people
5 Not only does illiteracy affect a person individually, (but) it also reduces

WRITING TASK

1 P **2** A **3** E **4** A **5** A **6** A

Plan

Possible answer:

Possible reasons to support free and equal education for all:

Reason 1: Improves people's health as they understand how to look after themselves and perhaps feel they have more to live for. This is passed on to children, and slowly, poor health due to poverty is eradicated. Also, family sizes are known to reduce.

Reason 2: Improves personal economic situation. People who are literate and educated can look for work that is better paid (and also less dangerous; physically demanding) and provide better for their families.

Reason 3: Improves economic situation. Countries develop greater GDP per capita and can produce more economically with the resources they have.

Conclusion: However, in practice it is difficult to provide education for all, and it is possible for health and poverty to impact on whether a child goes to school or not. Therefore, there is the opposite correlation.

UNIT 8 Change

Vocabulary preview

1

1 F **2** T **3** F **4** F **5** T **6** T **7** F **8** F

2

Possible answers:

1 A *business model* is an outline of a good business structure.
3 If you *drive a company forward*, you lead the company with a view for progression and success.
4 If you *empower* someone, you give that person a sense of power.
7 A *mentoring scheme* involves experienced people supporting and advising less experienced people.
8 If you *execute* a strategy, you carry it out.

READING Leadership and change management

Global reading

1

a Kotter's eight-step approach to change management
b Fisher's model of personal change
c Lewin's Unfreeze, Change, Refreeze model

2

1 F, they should keep innovating
2 T
3 F, 70% fail
4 F, their journeys are different

3

1 L, K **2** L, K **3** L **4** F
5 L, K **6** F **7** K **8** L, K, F

4

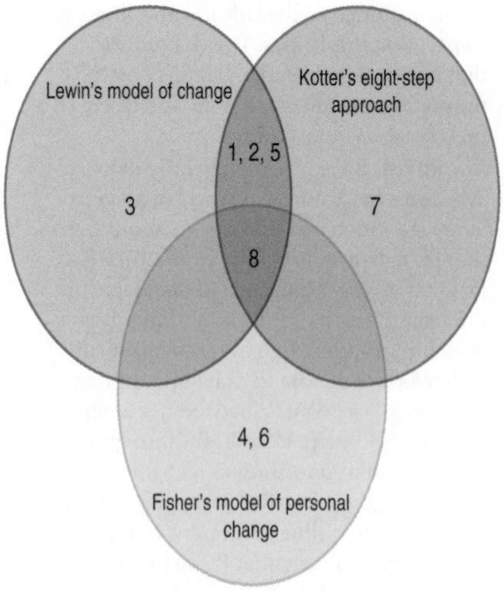

5

1 Admiring the view too long on a mountain without realizing there is more to climb.
2 An uphill struggle.
3 Melting a block of ice in one shape and refreezing it in another shape.
4 Crossing from one peak to another.

Critical thinking skill

1

… while other companies have mistakenly spent far too long looking at the scenery, not appreciating that further heights were there to be scaled.

2

The writer is critical of:

2 while other companies have mistakenly spent far too long looking at the scenery, not appreciating that further heights were there to be scaled.
4 It is the final stage which companies may struggle to apply in today's fast-moving world …
5 Yet one of the biggest reasons … / It is easy for a change management strategy to focus solely on systems, but …

The writer is not critical of:

1 Successful companies such as Apple®, Google, and Amazon are all examples of industry leaders which understand that they still have a mountain to climb, while …
6 … provides businesses with a comprehensive and solid understanding of how much of an impact change may have on employees across the board.

The writer is both critical and not critical of 3:
… planning and executing a change strategy can be an uphill struggle (not critical) with organisations often pulling the plug on strategies at the first sign of difficulty. (critical)

Language development: Idiomatic language

1

1 b **2** d **3** e **4** a **5** c

3

1 politely **2** not knowing **3** most
4 definitely **5** basic **6** changes
7 supporting **8** fail **9** more 10 easy

Language development: Participle clauses

1

1 Wanting to create a change strategy, senior managers brought in a consultant.
2 While reading the consultant's report, they realized they needed to organize a meeting.
3 Attended by all management, the meeting took place in the boardroom.
4 On hearing about the report, the managers had a lot of questions.

2

1 While/On hearing about the changes, some staff members became angry.
2 Some staff members resigned, wanting things to stay the same. / Wanting things to stay the same, some staff members resigned.
3 After explaining the situation, / Having explained the situation, managers received positive feedback from the staff.
4 Having received training, all staff successfully coped with the changes. / All staff, after receiving training, successfully coped with the changes.

Writing skill

1&2

Possible answer:

Buckson's supermarket

Introduction

Buckson's is a local grocery store located in a large residential area of the town. It first opened in 1924 and has been a family business ever since. Because sales have been dropping slowly for the last ten years, research has been conducted to find out the reasons why.

Research method

The research involved:
- Face-to-face interviews with 30 Buckson's customers.
- Face-to-face interviews with 30 customers of Buckson's closest rival supermarket, Shop Mart.

The interviews lasted approximately ten minutes and included 15 questions.

Results

The results of the research established that:
- Customers are purchasing fewer items due to long lines at the check-out, no Internet presence, and no delivery service.
- Customers believe Buckson's goods to be of high quality (e.g., bakery goods are freshly made). Several customers said, "They make the best cakes in town."
- Customers think the staff are friendlier and more helpful than at the nearest competitor.

Conclusions

Overall analysis of the results suggests that customers would be happy to pay Buckson's prices if they were able to receive faster check-out service and the opportunity to order food online or in the store which is later delivered.

Recommendations

It is highly recommended that Buckson's:
- Invest in a higher speed Internet connection and faster scanners to avoid long lines at the check-out.
- Create an online shopping facility, including a shopping app that can be downloaded onto mobile phones.
- Purchase vans in which food can be delivered.
- Ensure that current staff members are able to adapt to the new changes and continue to provide a high-quality service to customers.

WRITING TASK

Possible answer:

The purpose of the report is to make recommendations as to what the modernization program should involve.

STUDY SKILLS Editing your work

Scenario

Possible answer:

Faisal left time between writing his report and revising it. He checked that the information all led to his conclusions. However, he did not check that the report was structured in a way that readers could follow, he did not proofread it, and he did not leave enough time to revise the report effectively.

UNIT 9 Flow

Vocabulary preview

1

1 civilizations **2** soil **3** crops **4** Irrigation
5 commodities **6** domesticate **7** Trade
8 flourish

READING How rivers made civilisation

Global reading

1 All of these cultures arose from rivers.
2 The rivers flooded in these places, leaving behind fertile soil that was excellent for growing crops.
3 Disputes over water created a need for writing so that clear ownership records could be kept.
4 Some observers say that the sorrow and mourning found in ancient Mesopotamian literature can still be found in modern Iraqi culture today.
5 The Nile gave ancient Egyptians valuable commodities for trade while also serving as the trade route itself.
6 Because it was virtually impossible for an invading army to cross the desert, ancient Egypt enjoyed a stable government that was mostly free of war and conflict.

Critical thinking skill

2

1 c **2** a **3** b

3

1 confusing correlation and causation
2 after, therefore, because
3 argument from ignorance

Language development: Verbs and expressions with prepositions

1

1 had an effect on	**6** resulted in
2 arose from	**7** lead to
3 known as	**8** resulted from
4 made for	**9** gave rise to
5 made use of	

2

1 with **2** of **3** at **4** of **5** to **6** to

Language development: Expressing causality

1

1 The Nile's yearly floods gave rise to excellent farmland.
2 The development of money resulted in more efficient trade.
3 As Egypt was the strongest culture in the region, it dominated trade.
4 The gentle nature of the Nile's floods had an effect on the ancient Egyptians' outlook on life.
5 Water was scarce; consequently, conflict was common in Mesopotamia.
6 Political instability in Mesopotamia resulted from a lack of natural barriers to invasion.
7 Disputes over land were a factor in the development of writing and laws.
8 The impact of rivers on the rise of civilization is hard to overstate.

WRITING A cause and effect essay

Writing skill

1

The writer followed tips 1 and 2.

2

Possible answer:

Almost every part of our daily lives—from traffic laws to text messages to imported fruit and vegetables—has its roots in the early river valley civilisations. By taking advantage of the ideal conditions these rivers created for agriculture, trade, and—in the case of Egypt—unity and stability, these ancient peoples laid the foundations of our societies today: writing, laws, agriculture, calendars, trade, and much more. The history of these civilisations also highlights the importance of the environment to human societies; we still depend on rivers today and ought to treat them with greater care.

WRITING TASK

Possible answers:

Agriculture: The violent, unpredictable floods of the Yellow River created excellent farmland.
History and Politics: The river allowed people to travel between different communities; this united the different ethnic groups along the river.
Culture: Because they were surrounded by mountains and deserts, they were isolated from the world outside China.
Economics: Because the river was good for agriculture, it made the area the most prosperous region in China.

Answer key

CRITICAL THINKING SKILLS
Assuming a causal link

Passage 1: The assumed causal link: obesity leads to longer life expectancy. The link does not follow logically from the reasons given: it hasn't been shown that those who are obese live longer, nor why obesity should lead to longer life.
Passage 2: The assumed causal link: that it was the roof-top protest that led to the prisoners' release, rather than, for example, them having been found innocent, the evidence against them being found to be flawed, or them having completed their sentences. Something which has happened only twice does not establish a solid trend.
Passage 3: The assumed causal links: that the man was murdered, that somebody broke in to do this, and that the knife was the murder weapon. However, in actuality, no murder may have occurred.

UNIT 10 Conflict

Vocabulary preview

1 a **2** c **3** c **4** c **5** a **6** a **7** b **8** d

READING Culture and conflict

Global reading

1

1 low-context **2** high-context **3** polychronic **4** monochronic **5** diffuseness **6** specificity

2

Possible answers:

1. The writer is a high-context communicator, but his wife has a low-context style. Because of this, he couldn't clearly communicate his concerns about the dishes to his wife.
2. The Asian businessman comes from a high-context culture where nonverbal communication and long silences are common, and he misinterprets the low-context American's direct communication style for rudeness.
3. The British woman is from a monochronic culture where schedules are very important, whereas her South American friend has a polychronic view of time and does not see arriving late as a sign of rudeness.
4. The Middle Eastern businessman has a polychronic view of time and sees it as natural to delay a meeting in order to help his family, whereas the European has a monochronic outlook that values schedules above relationships.

3 .

1 paragraph 3 **2** paragraph 7 **3** paragraph 9 **4** paragraph 9

Critical thinking skill

1

1, 2, 4, and 6 are meant to be humorous.

Language development: Phrasal nouns

2

1 slowdown **2** build-up **3** outburst **4** breakup **5** drawback **6** runaround

3

Similar meanings: breakup, build-up, outburst, slowdown
Different meanings: drawback (verb = to move away from something; noun = disadvantage); runaround (verb = to run a circle around something; to be very busy doing different things; noun = a delay meant to evade or frustrate)
Different word order: outburst

Language development: Verb patterns

1

1 for hurting **2** about not being
3 someone to have **4** you to disagree
5 you of not listening **6** from criticizing
7 someone not to raise **8** someone for saying
9 from turning

WRITING Analyzing a conflict

Writing skill

1

Voice 1 would be better for an essay in a magazine; voice 2 would be better for an academic paper. We know this because the language in voice 1 is less formal than in voice 2.

WRITING TASK

The American anthropologist Edward T. Hall's concept of monochronic and polychronic time <u>is a valuable tool for understanding</u> the deeper roots of intercultural conflict. A prime example of this can be found in the difficulties that a U.S. clothing company recently <u>experienced while doing</u> business in South America. The company initially came to the region with a very monochronic view of time, in which <u>staying on schedule</u> was more important than <u>building relationships</u>. In his first visit, the sales rep spent only a few days in the area. As a result, the trip <u>caused him to feel</u> anxious, as the people he met <u>spent more time socializing</u> than apparently <u>doing business</u>. In actuality, the South American partners <u>saw socializing</u> as part of business.
The writer's voice is positive about using Hall's concept and critical of the company's approach to doing business in South America.